www.EffortlessMath.com

... So Much More Online!

✓ FREE Math lessons

✓ More Math learning books!

✓ Mathematics Worksheets

✓ Online Math Tutors

Need a PDF version of this book?

Please visit www.EffortlessMath.com

Pre-Algebra Study Guide 2020 - 2021

A Comprehensive Review and Step-By-Step Guide to Preparing for the Pre-Algebra

By

Reza Nazari & Ava Ross

All inquiries should be addressed to:

info@effortlessMath.com

www.EffortlessMath.com

ISBN: 978-1-64612-457-2

Published by: Effortless Math Education

www.EffortlessMath.com

Visit www.EffortlessMath.com

for Online Math Practice

Description

Pre-Algebra Study Guide is designed by top Algebra instructors and test prep experts to help test takers succeed on the Pre-Algebra Test. The updated version of this comprehensive Pre-Algebra preparation book includes Math lessons, extensive exercises, sample Pre-Algebra questions, and quizzes with answers and detailed solutions to help you hone your math skills, overcome your exam anxiety, boost your confidence—and do your best to ace the Pre-Algebra exam on test day. Upon completion of this perfect Pre-Algebra prep book, you will have a solid foundation and sufficient practice to ace the Pre-Algebra test.

Not only does this all-inclusive prep book offer everything you will ever need to prepare for the Pre-Algebra test, but it also contains abundant skill-building exercises to help you check your exam-readiness and identify where you need more practice.

Pre-Algebra Study Guide contains many exciting and unique features to help you prepare for the Pre-Algebra test, including:

- ✓ Content 100% aligned with the 2020 Pre-Algebra test
- ✓ Written by Algebra instructors and test experts
- ✓ Complete coverage of all Pre-Algebra concepts and topics which you will be tested
- ✓ Step-by-step guide for all Pre-Algebra topics
- ✓ Abundant Math skill building exercises to help test-takers approach different question types that might be unfamiliar to them
- ✓ Exercises on different Pre-Algebra topics such as integers, percent, equations, polynomials, exponents and radicals

This Pre-Algebra prep book and other Effortless Math Education books are used by thousands of students each year to help them review core content areas, brush-up in math, discover their strengths and weaknesses, and achieve their best scores on the Pre-Algebra test.

Contents

Description 1

Simplifying Fractions 6

Adding and Subtracting Fractions 8

Multiplying and Dividing Fractions 10

Adding Mixed Numbers 12

Subtracting Mixed Numbers 14

Multiplying Mixed Numbers 16

Dividing Mixed Numbers 18

Comparing Decimals 20

Rounding Decimals 22

Adding and Subtracting Decimals 24

Multiplying and Dividing Decimals 26

Adding and Subtracting Integers 28

Multiplying and Dividing Integers 30

Order of Operation 32

Integers and Absolute Value 34

Simplifying Ratios 36

Proportional Ratios 38

Create Proportion 40

Similarity and Ratios 42

Percent Problems 44

Percent of Increase and Decrease 46

Discount, Tax and Tip 48

Simple Interest 50

Simplifying Variable Expressions 52

Simplifying Polynomial Expressions 54

Evaluating One Variable 56

Evaluating Two Variables 58

The Distributive Property 60

One–Step Equations 62

System of Equations 66

Graphing Single–Variable Inequalities 68

One–Step Inequalities 70

Multi –Step Inequalities 72

Finding Slope 74

Graphing Lines Using Slope–Intercept Form 76

Writing Linear Equations.. 78

Finding Midpoint... 80

Finding Distance of Two Points.. 82

Multiplication Property of Exponents.. 84

Division Property of Exponents... 86

Powers of Products and Quotients 88

Zero and Negative Exponents 90

Negative Exponents and Negative Bases 92

Scientific Notation... 94

Radicals 96

Simplifying Polynomials 98

Adding and Subtracting Polynomials 100

Multiplying Binomials 102

Multiplying and Dividing Monomials.. 104

Multiplying a Polynomial and a Monomial 106

Multiplying Monomials... 108

Factoring Trinomials 110

The Pythagorean Theorem 112

Triangles.. 114

Polygons.. 116

Circles.. 118

Cubes... 120

Trapezoids... 122

Rectangular Prisms... 124

Cylinder 126

Mean, Median, Mode, and Range of the Given Data 128

Probability Problems... 130

Pie Graph 132

Permutations and Combinations 134

Name:	Date: ....

Topic	**Simplifying Fractions**	
Notes	✓ Evenly divide both the top and bottom of the fraction by $2, 3, 5, 7, \ldots$ etc. ✓ Continue until you can't go any further.	
Example	**Simplify** $\frac{36}{48}$ To simplify $\frac{36}{48}$, find a number that both 36 and 48 are divisible by. Both are divisible by 12. Then: $\frac{36}{48} = \frac{36 \div 12}{48 \div 12} = \frac{3}{4}$	
Your Turn!	1) $\frac{2}{18} =$	2) $\frac{22}{66} =$
	3) $\frac{12}{48} =$	4) $\frac{11}{99} =$
	5) $\frac{15}{75} =$	6) $\frac{25}{100} =$
	7) $\frac{16}{72} =$	8) $\frac{32}{96} =$
	9) $\frac{14}{77} =$	10) $\frac{60}{84} =$

Name:	Date: ....

Topic	**Simplifying Fractions - Answers**	
Notes	✓ Evenly divide both the top and bottom of the fraction by 2, 3, 5, 7, ... etc. ✓ Continue until you can't go any further.	
Example	**Simplify** $\frac{36}{48}$ To simplify $\frac{36}{48}$, find a number that both 36 and 48 are divisible by. Both are divisible by 12. Then: $\frac{36}{48} = \frac{36 \div 12}{48 \div 12} = \frac{3}{4}$	
Your Turn!	1) $\frac{2}{18} = \frac{1}{9}$	2) $\frac{22}{66} = \frac{1}{3}$
	3) $\frac{12}{48} = \frac{1}{4}$	4) $\frac{11}{99} = \frac{1}{9}$
	5) $\frac{15}{75} = \frac{1}{5}$	6) $\frac{25}{100} = \frac{1}{4}$
	7) $\frac{16}{72} = \frac{2}{9}$	8) $\frac{32}{96} = \frac{1}{3}$
	9) $\frac{14}{77} = \frac{2}{11}$	10) $\frac{60}{84} = \frac{5}{7}$

Name:	Date: ....

Topic	**Adding and Subtracting Fractions**
Notes	✓ For "like" fractions (fractions with the same denominator), add or subtract the numerators and write the answer over the common denominator. ✓ Find equivalent fractions with the same denominator before you can add or subtract fractions with different denominators. ✓ Adding and Subtracting with the same denominator: $$\frac{a}{b}+\frac{c}{b}=\frac{a+c}{b}\ ,\frac{a}{b}-\frac{c}{b}=\frac{a-c}{b}$$ ✓ Adding and Subtracting fractions with different denominators: $$\frac{a}{b}+\frac{c}{d}=\frac{ad+bc}{bd},\frac{a}{b}-\frac{c}{d}=\frac{ad-bc}{bd}$$
Example	*Find the sum.* $\frac{3}{5}+\frac{2}{3}=\frac{(3)3+(5)(2)}{5\times3}=\frac{19}{15}$ *Subtract.* $\frac{4}{7}-\frac{3}{7}=\frac{1}{7}$
Your Turn!	1) $\frac{3}{5}+\frac{2}{7}=$ 2) $\frac{7}{9}-\frac{4}{7}=$ 3) $\frac{4}{9}+\frac{5}{8}=$ 4) $\frac{5}{8}-\frac{2}{5}=$ 5) $\frac{2}{5}+\frac{1}{6}=$ 6) $\frac{2}{3}-\frac{1}{4}=$ 7) $\frac{8}{9}+\frac{5}{7}=$ 8) $\frac{6}{7}-\frac{5}{9}=$

www.EffortlessMath.com

| Name: .... | Date: .... |

Topic	**Adding and Subtracting Fractions - Answers**
Notes	✓ For "like" fractions (fractions with the same denominator), add or subtract the numerators and write the answer over the common denominator. ✓ Find equivalent fractions with the same denominator before you can add or subtract fractions with different denominators. ✓ Adding and Subtracting with the same denominator: $$\frac{a}{b} + \frac{c}{b} = \frac{a+c}{b}, \quad \frac{a}{b} - \frac{c}{b} = \frac{a-c}{b}$$ ✓ Adding and Subtracting fractions with different denominators: $$\frac{a}{b} + \frac{c}{d} = \frac{ad+bc}{bd}, \frac{a}{b} - \frac{c}{d} = \frac{ad-bc}{bd}$$
Example	**Find the sum.** $\frac{3}{5} + \frac{2}{3} = \frac{(3)3+(5)(2)}{5 \times 3} = \frac{19}{15}$ **Subtract.** $\frac{4}{7} - \frac{3}{7} = \frac{1}{7}$
Your Turn!	1) $\frac{3}{5} + \frac{2}{7} = \frac{31}{35}$ 2) $\frac{7}{9} - \frac{4}{7} = \frac{13}{63}$ 3) $\frac{4}{9} + \frac{5}{8} = \frac{77}{72}$ 4) $\frac{5}{8} - \frac{2}{5} = \frac{9}{40}$ 5) $\frac{2}{5} + \frac{1}{6} = \frac{17}{30}$ 6) $\frac{2}{3} - \frac{1}{4} = \frac{5}{12}$ 7) $\frac{8}{9} + \frac{5}{7} = \frac{101}{63}$ 8) $\frac{6}{7} - \frac{5}{9} = \frac{19}{63}$

Name:	Date: ....

Topic	**Multiplying and Dividing Fractions**	
Notes	✓ Multiplying fractions: multiply the top numbers and multiply the bottom numbers. ✓ Dividing fractions: Keep, Change, Flip Keep first fraction, change division sign to multiplication, and flip the numerator and denominator of the second fraction. Then, solve!	
Examples	*Multiply.* $\frac{2}{5} \times \frac{3}{4} =$ Multiply the top numbers and multiply the bottom numbers. $\frac{2}{5} \times \frac{3}{4} = \frac{2\times3}{5\times4} = \frac{6}{20}$, simplify: $\frac{6}{2} = \frac{6\div2}{20\div2} = \frac{3}{10}$ *Divide.* $\frac{2}{5} \div \frac{3}{4} =$ Keep first fraction, change division sign to multiplication, and flip the numerator and denominator of the second fraction. Then: $\frac{2}{5} \div \frac{3}{4} = \frac{2}{5} \times \frac{4}{3} = \frac{2\times4}{5\times3} = \frac{8}{15}$	
Your Turn!	1) $\frac{5}{9} \times \frac{4}{7} =$	2) $\frac{3}{5} \div \frac{2}{3} =$
	3) $\frac{2}{7} \times \frac{3}{5} =$	4) $\frac{2}{5} \div \frac{7}{12} =$
	5) $\frac{1}{7} \times \frac{4}{9} =$	6) $\frac{2}{9} \div \frac{3}{7} =$
	7) $\frac{2}{5} \times \frac{6}{7} =$	8) $\frac{1}{4} \div \frac{2}{5} =$

| **Name:** .... | **Date:** .... |

Topic	**Multiplying and Dividing Fractions - Answers**
Notes	✓ Multiplying fractions: multiply the top numbers and multiply the bottom numbers. ✓ Dividing fractions: Keep, Change, Flip Keep first fraction, change division sign to multiplication, and flip the numerator and denominator of the second fraction. Then, solve!

Examples	*Multiply.* $\frac{2}{5} \times \frac{3}{4} =$ Multiply the top numbers and multiply the bottom numbers. $\frac{2}{5} \times \frac{3}{4} = \frac{2 \times 3}{5 \times 4} = \frac{6}{20}$, simplify: $\frac{6}{2} = \frac{6 \div 2}{20 \div 2} = \frac{3}{10}$ *Divide.* $\frac{2}{5} \div \frac{3}{4} =$ Keep first fraction, change division sign to multiplication, and flip the numerator and denominator of the second fraction. Then: $\frac{2}{5} \div \frac{3}{4} = \frac{2}{5} \times \frac{4}{3} = \frac{2 \times 4}{5 \times 3} = \frac{8}{15}$

Your Turn!	1) $\frac{5}{9} \times \frac{4}{7} = \frac{20}{63}$	2) $\frac{3}{5} \div \frac{2}{3} = \frac{9}{10}$
	3) $\frac{2}{7} \times \frac{3}{5} = \frac{6}{35}$	4) $\frac{2}{5} \div \frac{7}{12} = \frac{24}{35}$
	5) $\frac{1}{7} \times \frac{4}{9} = \frac{4}{63}$	6) $\frac{2}{9} \div \frac{3}{7} = \frac{14}{27}$
	7) $\frac{2}{5} \times \frac{6}{7} = \frac{12}{35}$	8) $\frac{1}{4} \div \frac{2}{5} = \frac{5}{8}$

| Name: .... | Date: .... |

Topic	**Adding Mixed Numbers**
Notes	Use the following steps for adding mixed numbers. ✓ Add whole numbers of the mixed numbers. ✓ Add the fractions of each mixed number. ✓ Find the Least Common Denominator (LCD) if necessary. ✓ Add whole numbers and fractions. ✓ Write your answer in lowest terms.
Example	***Add mixed numbers.*** $1\frac{1}{2} + 2\frac{2}{3} =$ Rewriting our equation with parts separated, $1 + \frac{1}{2} + 2 + \frac{2}{3}$ Add whole numbers: $1 + 2 = 3$ Add fractions: $\frac{1}{2} + \frac{2}{3} = \frac{3}{6} + \frac{4}{6} = \frac{7}{6} = 1\frac{1}{6}$, Now, combine the whole and fraction parts: $3 + 1 + \frac{1}{6} = 4\frac{1}{6}$

Your Turn!	1) $1\frac{1}{12} + 2\frac{3}{4} =$	2) $3\frac{5}{8} + 1\frac{1}{4} =$
	3) $1\frac{1}{10} + 2\frac{2}{5} =$	4) $2\frac{5}{6} + 2\frac{2}{9} =$
	5) $2\frac{2}{7} + 1\frac{2}{21} =$	6) $1\frac{3}{8} + 3\frac{2}{3} =$
	7) $3\frac{1}{5} + 1\frac{2}{8} =$	8) $3\frac{1}{2} + 2\frac{3}{7} =$

| Name: .... | Date: .... |

Topic	**Adding Mixed Numbers - Answers**
Notes	Use the following steps for adding mixed numbers. ✓ Add whole numbers of the mixed numbers. ✓ Add the fractions of each mixed number. ✓ Find the Least Common Denominator (LCD) if necessary. ✓ Add whole numbers and fractions. ✓ Write your answer in lowest terms.
Example	**Add mixed numbers.** $1\frac{1}{2} + 2\frac{2}{3} =$ Rewriting our equation with parts separated, $1 + \frac{1}{2} + 2 + \frac{2}{3}$ Add whole numbers: $1 + 2 = 3$ Add fractions: $\frac{1}{2} + \frac{2}{3} = \frac{3}{6} + \frac{4}{6} = \frac{7}{6} = 1\frac{1}{6}$ Now, combine the whole and fraction parts: $3 + 1 + \frac{1}{6} = 4\frac{1}{6}$
Your Turn!	1) $1\frac{1}{12} + 2\frac{3}{4} = 3\frac{5}{6}$ 2) $3\frac{5}{8} + 1\frac{1}{4} = 4\frac{7}{8}$ 3) $1\frac{1}{10} + 2\frac{2}{5} = 3\frac{1}{2}$ 4) $2\frac{5}{6} + 2\frac{2}{9} = 5\frac{1}{18}$ 5) $2\frac{2}{7} + 1\frac{2}{21} = 3\frac{8}{21}$ 6) $1\frac{3}{8} + 3\frac{2}{3} = 5\frac{1}{24}$ 7) $3\frac{1}{5} + 1\frac{2}{8} = 4\frac{9}{20}$ 8) $3\frac{1}{2} + 2\frac{3}{7} = 5\frac{13}{14}$

Name:	Date: ....

Topic	**Subtracting Mixed Numbers**
Notes	Use the following steps for subtracting mixed numbers. ✓ Convert mixed numbers into improper fractions. $a\frac{c}{b} = \frac{ab+c}{b}$ ✓ Find equivalent fractions with the same denominator for unlike fractions (fractions with different denominators) ✓ Subtract the second fraction from the first one. ✓ Write your answer in lowest terms and convert it into a mixed number if the answer is an improper fraction.
Example	**Subtract.** $5\frac{1}{2} - 2\frac{2}{3} =$ Convert mixed numbers into fractions: $5\frac{1}{2} = \frac{5\times 2 + 1}{5} = \frac{11}{2}$ and $2\frac{2}{3} = \frac{2\times 3 + 2}{4} = \frac{8}{3}$, these two fractions are "unlike" fractions. (they have different denominators). Find equivalent fractions with the same denominator. Use this formula: $\frac{a}{b} - \frac{c}{d} = \frac{ad \;\; bc}{bd}$ $\frac{11}{2} - \frac{8}{3} = \frac{(11)(3)-(2)(8)}{2\times 3} = \frac{33-16}{6} = \frac{17}{6}$, the answer is an improper fraction, convert it into a mixed number. $\qquad \frac{17}{6} = 2\frac{5}{6}$

Your Turn!	
1) $2\frac{2}{5} - 1\frac{1}{3} =$	2) $3\frac{5}{8} - 2\frac{1}{3} =$
3) $6\frac{1}{4} - 1\frac{2}{7} =$	4) $8\frac{2}{3} - 1\frac{1}{4} =$
5) $8\frac{3}{4} - 1\frac{3}{8} =$	6) $2\frac{3}{8} - 1\frac{2}{3} =$
7) $13\frac{2}{7} - 1\frac{2}{21} =$	8) $5\frac{1}{2} - 2\frac{3}{7} =$

Name:	Date: ....

Topic	**Subtracting Mixed Numbers - Answers**
Notes	Use the following steps for subtracting mixed numbers. ✓ Convert mixed numbers into improper fractions. $a\frac{c}{b} = \frac{ab+c}{b}$ ✓ Find equivalent fractions with the same denominator for unlike fractions (fractions with different denominators) ✓ Subtract the second fraction from the first one. ✓ Write your answer in lowest terms and convert it into a mixed number if the answer is an improper fraction.
Example	***Subtract.*** $5\frac{1}{2} - 2\frac{2}{3} =$ Convert mixed numbers into fractions: $5\frac{1}{2} = \frac{5\times2+1}{5} = \frac{11}{2}$ and $2\frac{2}{3} = \frac{2\times3+2}{4} = \frac{8}{3}$, these two fractions are "unlike" fractions. (they have different denominators). Find equivalent fractions with the same denominator. Use this formula: $\frac{a}{b} - \frac{c}{d} = \frac{ad-bc}{bd}$ $\frac{11}{2} - \frac{8}{3} = \frac{(11)(3)-(2)(8)}{2\times3} = \frac{33-16}{6} = \frac{17}{6}$, the answer is an improper fraction, convert it into a mixed number. $\qquad \frac{17}{6} = 2\frac{5}{6}$

Your Turn!	1) $2\frac{2}{5} - 1\frac{1}{3} = 1\frac{1}{15}$	2) $3\frac{5}{8} - 2\frac{1}{3} = 1\frac{7}{24}$
	3) $6\frac{1}{4} - 1\frac{2}{7} = 4\frac{27}{28}$	4) $8\frac{2}{3} - 1\frac{1}{4} = 7\frac{5}{12}$
	5) $8\frac{3}{4} - 1\frac{3}{8} = 7\frac{3}{8}$	6) $2\frac{3}{8} - 1\frac{2}{3} = \frac{17}{24}$
	7) $13\frac{2}{7} - 1\frac{2}{21} = 12\frac{4}{21}$	8) $5\frac{1}{2} - 2\frac{3}{7} = 3\frac{1}{14}$

Name:	Date: ....

Topic	**Multiplying Mixed Numbers**
Notes	✓ Convert the mixed numbers into fractions. $a\frac{c}{b} = a + \frac{c}{b} = \frac{ab+c}{b}$ ✓ Multiply fractions and simplify if necessary. $\frac{a}{b} \times \frac{c}{d} = \frac{a \times c}{b \times d}$ ✓ If the answer is an improper fraction (numerator is bigger than denominator), convert it into a mixed number.
Example	**Multiply** $2\frac{1}{4} \times 3\frac{1}{2}$ Convert mixed numbers into fractions: $2\frac{1}{4} = \frac{2 \times 4 + 1}{4} = \frac{9}{4}$ and $3\frac{1}{2} = \frac{3 \times 2 + 1}{2} = \frac{7}{2}$ Multiply two fractions: $\frac{9}{4} \times \frac{7}{2} = \frac{9 \times 7}{4 \times 2} = \frac{63}{8}$ The answer is an improper fraction. Convert it into a mixed number: $$\frac{63}{8} = 7\frac{7}{8}$$
Your Turn!	1) $5\frac{2}{3} \times 2\frac{2}{9} =$ 2) $4\frac{1}{6} \times 5\frac{3}{7} =$ 3) $3\frac{1}{3} \times 3\frac{3}{4} =$ 4) $2\frac{2}{9} \times 6\frac{1}{3} =$ 5) $2\frac{2}{7} \times 4\frac{3}{5} =$ 6) $1\frac{4}{7} \times 9\frac{1}{2} =$ 7) $4\frac{1}{8} \times 3\frac{2}{3} =$ 8) $6\frac{2}{3} \times 1\frac{1}{4} =$

| Name: .... | Date: .... |

Topic	**Multiplying Mixed Numbers - Answers**
Notes	✓ Convert the mixed numbers into fractions. $a\frac{c}{b} = a + \frac{c}{b} = \frac{ab+c}{b}$ ✓ Multiply fractions and simplify if necessary. $\frac{a}{b} \times \frac{c}{d} = \frac{a \times c}{b \times d}$ ✓ If the answer is an improper fraction (numerator is bigger than denominator), convert it into a mixed number.
Example	**Multiply** $2\frac{1}{4} \times 3\frac{1}{2}$ Convert mixed numbers into fractions: $2\frac{1}{4} = \frac{2 \times 4 + 1}{4} = \frac{9}{4}$ and $3\frac{1}{2} = \frac{3 \times 2 + 1}{2} = \frac{7}{2}$ Multiply two fractions: $\frac{9}{4} \times \frac{7}{2} = \frac{9 \times 7}{4 \times 2} = \frac{63}{8}$ The answer is an improper fraction. Convert it into a mixed number: $$\frac{63}{8} = 7\frac{7}{8}$$
Your Turn!	1) $5\frac{2}{3} \times 2\frac{2}{9} = 12\frac{16}{27}$ 2) $4\frac{1}{6} \times 5\frac{3}{7} = 22\frac{13}{21}$ 3) $3\frac{1}{3} \times 3\frac{3}{4} = 12\frac{1}{2}$ 4) $2\frac{2}{9} \times 6\frac{1}{3} = 14\frac{2}{27}$ 5) $2\frac{2}{7} \times 4\frac{3}{5} = 10\frac{18}{35}$ 6) $1\frac{4}{7} \times 9\frac{1}{2} = 14\frac{13}{14}$ 7) $4\frac{1}{8} \times 3\frac{2}{3} = 15\frac{1}{8}$ 8) $6\frac{2}{3} \times 1\frac{1}{4} = 8\frac{1}{3}$

Name: ....   **Date:** ....

Topic	Dividing Mixed Numbers
Notes	✓ Convert the mixed numbers into improper fractions. $$a\frac{c}{b} = a + \frac{c}{b} = \frac{ab + c}{b}$$ ✓ Divide fractions and simplify if necessary.
Example	*Solve.* $2\frac{1}{3} \div 1\frac{1}{4} =$ Converting mixed numbers to fractions: $2\frac{1}{3} \div 1\frac{1}{4} = \frac{7}{3} \div \frac{5}{4}$ Keep, Change, Flip: $\frac{7}{3} \div \frac{5}{4} = \frac{7}{3} \times \frac{4}{5} = \frac{7 \times 4}{3 \times 5} = \frac{28}{15} = 1\frac{13}{15}$
Your Turn!	1) $3\frac{2}{7} \div 2\frac{1}{4} =$ 2) $4\frac{2}{9} \div 1\frac{5}{6} =$ 3) $4\frac{2}{3} \div 3\frac{2}{5} =$ 4) $5\frac{4}{5} \div 4\frac{3}{4} =$ 5) $1\frac{8}{9} \div 2\frac{3}{7} =$ 6) $3\frac{3}{8} \div 2\frac{2}{5} =$ 7) $4\frac{1}{5} \div 3\frac{1}{9} =$ 8) $4\frac{2}{3} \div 1\frac{8}{9} =$ 9) $5\frac{2}{3} \div 3\frac{3}{7} =$ 10) $7\frac{1}{2} \div 5\frac{1}{3} =$

| Name: .... | Date: .... |

Topic	**Dividing Mixed Numbers- Answers**
Notes	✓ Convert the mixed numbers into improper fractions. $$a\frac{c}{b} = a + \frac{c}{b} = \frac{ab + c}{b}$$ ✓ Divide fractions and simplify if necessary.
Example	***Solve.*** $2\frac{1}{3} \div 1\frac{1}{4} =$ Converting mixed numbers to fractions: $2\frac{1}{3} \div 1\frac{1}{4} = \frac{7}{3} \div \frac{5}{4}$ Keep, Change, Flip: $\frac{7}{3} \div \frac{5}{4} = \frac{7}{3} \times \frac{4}{5} = \frac{7 \times 4}{3 \times 5} = \frac{28}{15} = 1\frac{13}{15}$

Your Turn!	1) $3\frac{2}{7} \div 2\frac{1}{4} = 1\frac{29}{63}$	2) $4\frac{2}{9} \div 1\frac{5}{6} = 2\frac{10}{33}$
	3) $4\frac{2}{3} \div 3\frac{2}{5} = 1\frac{19}{51}$	4) $5\frac{4}{5} \div 4\frac{3}{4} = 1\frac{21}{95}$
	5) $1\frac{8}{9} \div 2\frac{3}{7} = \frac{7}{9}$	6) $3\frac{3}{8} \div 2\frac{2}{5} = 1\frac{13}{32}$
	7) $4\frac{1}{5} \div 3\frac{1}{9} = 1\frac{7}{20}$	8) $4\frac{2}{3} \div 1\frac{8}{9} = 2\frac{8}{17}$
	9) $5\frac{2}{3} \div 3\frac{3}{7} = 1\frac{47}{72}$	10) $7\frac{1}{2} \div 5\frac{1}{3} = 1\frac{13}{32}$

Name:	Date: ....

Topic	**Comparing Decimals**
Notes	Decimals: is a fraction written in a special form. For example, instead of writing $\frac{1}{2}$ you can write **0.5**. For comparing decimals: ✓ Compare each digit of two decimals in the same place value. ✓ Start from left. Compare hundreds, tens, ones, tenth, hundredth, etc. ✓ To compare numbers, use these symbols: - Equal to =,　　　　　　Less than <,　Greater than > Greater than or equal ≥,　　Less than or equal ≤
Examples	**Compare 0.40 and 0.04.** 0.40 *is greater than* 0.04, because the tenth place of 0.40 is 4, but the tenth place of 0.04 is zero. Then: $0.40 > 0.04$ **Compare 0.0912 and 0.912.** 0.912 *is greater than* 0.0912, because the tenth place of 0.912 is 9, but the tenth place of 0.0912 is zero. Then: $0.0912 < 0.912$
Your Turn!	1) 0.91 ☐ 0.95 　　　　 2) 1.79 ☐ 1.80 3) 19.1 ☐ 19.09 　　　　 4) 2.45 ☐ 2.089 5) 1.258 ☐ 12.58 　　　　 6) 0.89 ☐ 0.890 7) 3.871 ☐ 2.998 　　　　 8) 0.567 ☐ 0.756

Name:	Date: ....

Topic	**Comparing Decimals - Answers**	

Notes	Decimals: is a fraction written in a special form. For example, instead of writing $\frac{1}{2}$ you can write **0.5**.
	
	For comparing decimals:
	
	✓ Compare each digit of two decimals in the same place value.
	✓ Start from left. Compare hundreds, tens, ones, tenth, hundredth, etc.
	✓ To compare numbers, use these symbols:
	  - Equal to $=$, Less than $<$, Greater than $>$
	   Greater than or equal $\geq$, Less than or equal $\leq$	

Examples	***Compare 0.40 and 0.04.*** 0.40 *is greater than* 0.04, because the tenth place of 0.40 is 4, but the tenth place of 0.04 is zero. Then: $0.40 > 0.04$ ***Compare 0.0912 and 0.912.*** 0.912 *is greater than* 0.0912, because the tenth place of 0.912 is 9, but the tenth place of 0.0912 is zero. Then: $0.0912 < 0.912$	
Your Turn!	1) $0.91 < 0.95$	2) $1.78 < 1.80$
	3) $19.1 > 19.09$	4) $2.45 > 2.089$
	5) $1.258 < 12.58$	6) $0.89 = 0.890$
	7) $3.387 > 2.998$	8) $0.567 < 0.756$

| Name: .... | Date: .... |

Topic	**Rounding Decimals**

Notes	✓ We can round decimals to a certain accuracy or number of decimal places.
	✓ Let's review place values: For example:
	 35.4817
	    3: tens 5: ones 4: tenths
	
	   8: hundredths 1: thousandths 7:tens thousandths
	
	✓ To round a decimal, find the place value you'll round to.
	✓ Find the digit to the right of the place value you're rounding to.
	If it is 5 or bigger, add 1 to the place value you're rounding to and remove all digits on its right side. If the digit to the right of the place value is less than 5, keep the place value and remove all digits on the right.

Example	***Round 12.8365 to the hundredth place value.*** First look at the next place value to the right, (thousandths). It's 6 and it is greater than 5. Thus add 1 to the digit in the hundredth place. It is 3. → $3 + 1 = 4$, then, the answer is 12.84
Your Turn!	***Round each number to the underlined place value.*** 1) 32.5$\underline{4}$8 = 2) 2.3$\underline{2}$6 = 3) 55.$\underline{4}$23 = 4) 2$\underline{5}$.62 = 5) 11.$\underline{2}$65 = 6) 33.5$\underline{0}$5 = 7) 3.5$\underline{8}$9 = 8) 8.0$\underline{1}$9 =

Name:	**Date:** ....

Topic	**Rounding Decimals - Answers**
Notes	✓ We can round decimals to a certain accuracy or number of decimal places. ✓ Let's review place values: For example: $$35.4817$$ 3: tens 5: ones 4: tenths 8: hundredths 1: thousandths 7:tens thousandths ✓ To round a decimal, find the place value you'll round to. ✓ Find the digit to the right of the place value you're rounding to. If it is 5 or bigger, add 1 to the place value you're rounding to and remove all digits on its right side. If the digit to the right of the place value is less than 5, keep the place value and remove all digits on the right.
Example	**Round 12.8365 to the hundredth place value.** First look at the next place value to the right, (thousandths). It's 6 and it is greater than 5. Thus add 1 to the digit in the hundredth place. It is 3. → $3 + 1 = 4$, then, the answer is 12.84
Your Turn!	**Round each number to the underlined place value.** 1) $32.5\underline{4}8 = 32.55$ 2) $2.3\underline{2}6 = 2.33$ 3) $55.\underline{4}23 = 55.4$ 4) $2\underline{5}.62 = 26$ 5) $11.\underline{2}65 = 11.3$ 6) $33.5\underline{0}5 = 33.51$ 7) $3.5\underline{8}9 = 3.59$ 8) $8.0\underline{1}9 = 8.02$

Name:	Date: ....

Topic	**Adding and Subtracting Decimals**
Notes	✓ Line up the numbers. ✓ Add zeros to have same number of digits for both numbers if necessary. ✓ Add or subtract using column addition or subtraction.
Examples	***Add.*** $2.6 + 5.33 =$ First line up the numbers: $\begin{array}{r} 2.6 \\ +\,5.33 \\ \hline \end{array}$ →Add zeros to have same number of digits for both numbers. $\begin{array}{r} 2.60 \\ +\,5.33 \\ \hline \end{array}$ → Start with the hundredths place. $0 + 3 = 2$, $\begin{array}{r} 2.60 \\ +\,5.33 \\ \hline 3 \end{array}$ → Continue with tenths place. $6 + 3 = 9$, $\begin{array}{r} 2.60 \\ +\,5.33 \\ \hline .93 \end{array}$ → Add the ones place. $2 + 5 = 7$, $\begin{array}{r} 2.60 \\ +\,5.33 \\ \hline 7.93 \end{array}$ ***Subtract.*** $4.79 - 3.13 =$ $\begin{array}{r} 4.79 \\ -\,3.13 \\ \hline \end{array}$ Start with the hundredths place. $9 - 3 = 6$, $\begin{array}{r} 4.79 \\ -\,3.13 \\ \hline 6 \end{array}$, continue with tenths place. $7 - 1 = 6$, $\begin{array}{r} 4.79 \\ -\,3.13 \\ \hline .66 \end{array}$, subtract the ones place. $4 - 3 = 1$, $\begin{array}{r} 4.79 \\ -\,3.13 \\ \hline 1.66 \end{array}$
Your Turn!	1) $48.13 + 20.15 =$ 2) $78.14 - 65.19 =$ 3) $38.19 + 24.18 =$ 4) $57.26 - 43.54 =$ 5) $27.89 + 46.13 =$ 6) $49.65 - 32.78 =$

| Name: .... | Date: .... |

Topic	**Adding and Subtracting Decimals - Answers**
Notes	✓ Line up the numbers. ✓ Add zeros to have same number of digits for both numbers if necessary. ✓ Add or subtract using column addition or subtraction.
Examples	**Add**. $2.6 + 5.33 =$ First line up the numbers: $\begin{array}{r} 2.6 \\ +\,5.33 \\ \hline \end{array}$ →Add zeros to have same number of digits for both numbers. $\begin{array}{r} 2.60 \\ +\,5.33 \\ \hline \end{array}$ → Start with the hundredths place. $0 + 3 = 2$, $\begin{array}{r} 2.60 \\ +\,5.33 \\ \hline 3 \end{array}$ → Continue with tenths place. $6 + 3 = 9$, $\begin{array}{r} 2.60 \\ +\,5.33 \\ \hline .93 \end{array}$ → Add the ones place. $2 + 5 = 7$, $\begin{array}{r} 2.60 \\ +\,5.33 \\ \hline 7.93 \end{array}$ **Subtract**. $4.79 - 3.13 =$ $\begin{array}{r} 4.79 \\ -\,3.13 \\ \hline \end{array}$ Start with the hundredths place. $9 - 3 = 6$, $\begin{array}{r} 4.79 \\ -\,3.13 \\ \hline 6 \end{array}$, continue with tenths place. $7 - 1 = 6$, $\begin{array}{r} 4.79 \\ -\,3.13 \\ \hline .66 \end{array}$, subtract the ones place. $4 - 3 = 1$, $\begin{array}{r} 4.79 \\ -\,3.13 \\ \hline 1.66 \end{array}$
Your Turn!	1) $48.13 + 20.15 = 68.28$ 2) $78.14 - 65.19 = 12.95$ 3) $38.19 + 24.18 = 62.37$ 4) $57.26 - 43.54 = 13.72$ 5) $27.89 + 46.13 = 74.02$ 6) $49.65 - 32.78 = 16.87$

Name:	Date: ....

Topic	**Multiplying and Dividing Decimals**
Notes	For Multiplication: ✓ Ignore the decimal point and set up and multiply the numbers as you do with whole numbers. ✓ Count the total number of decimal places in both factors. ✓ Place the decimal point in the product. For Division: ✓ If the divisor is not a whole number, move decimal point to right to make it a whole number. Do the same for dividend. ✓ Divide similar to whole numbers.
Examples	***Find the product.*** $1.2 \times 2.3 =$ Set up and multiply the numbers as you do with whole numbers. Line up the numbers: $\begin{array}{r} \overset{12}{12} \\ \times 23 \end{array} \rightarrow$ Multiply: $\begin{array}{r} \overset{12}{\times 23} \\ \hline 276 \end{array} \rightarrow$ Count the total number of decimal places in both of the factors. There are two decimal digits. Then: $1.2 \times 2.3 = 2.76$ ***Find the quotient.*** $5.6 \div 0.8 =$ The divisor is not a whole number. Multiply it by 10 to get 8. $\rightarrow 0.8 \times 10 = 8$ Do the same for the dividend to get $56 \rightarrow 5.6 \times 10 = 56$ Now, divide: $56 \div 8 = 7$. The answer is 7.

Your Turn!	1) $1.13 \times 0.7 =$	2) $48.8 \div 8 =$
	3) $0.9 \times 0.68 =$	4) $66.8 \div 0.2 =$
	5) $0.18 \times 0.5 =$	6) $37.2 \div 100 =$

| Name: .... | Date: .... |

Topic	**Multiplying and Dividing Decimals - Answers**
Notes	For Multiplication: ✓ Ignore the decimal point and set up and multiply the numbers as you do with whole numbers. ✓ Count the total number of decimal places in both factors. ✓ Place the decimal point in the product. For Division: ✓ If the divisor is not a whole number, move decimal point to right to make it a whole number. Do the same for dividend. ✓ Divide similar to whole numbers.
Examples	**Find the product.** $1.2 \times 2.3 =$ Set up and multiply the numbers as you do with whole numbers. Line up the numbers: $\begin{array}{r} 12 \\ \times\,23 \\ \hline \end{array} \to$ Multiply: $\begin{array}{r} 12 \\ \times\,23 \\ \hline 276 \end{array} \to$ Count the total number of decimal places in both of the factors. There are two decimal digits. Then: $1.2 \times 2.3 = 2.76$ **Find the quotient.** $5.6 \div 0.8 =$ The divisor is not a whole number. Multiply it by 10 to get 8. → $0.8 \times 10 = 8$ Do the same for the dividend to get $56 \to 5.6 \times 10 = 56$ Now, divide: $56 \div 8 = 7$. The answer is 7.

Your Turn!	1) $1.13 \times 0.7 = 0.791$	2) $48.8 \div 8 = 6.1$
	3) $0.9 \times 0.68 = 0.612$	4) $66.8 \div 0.2 = 334$
	5) $0.18 \times 0.5 = 0.09$	6) $37.2 \div 100 = 0.372$

Name:	Date: ....

Topic	**Adding and Subtracting Integers**	
Notes	✓ Integers include: zero, counting numbers, and the negative of the counting numbers. $\{ \ldots, -3, -2, -1, 0, 1, 2, 3, \ldots \}$ ✓ Add a positive integer by moving to the right on the number line. ✓ Add a negative integer by moving to the left on the number line. Subtract an integer by adding its opposite.	
Examples	***Solve***. $(4) - (-8) =$ Keep the first number and convert the sign of the second number to its opposite. (change subtraction into addition. Then: $(4) + 8 = 12$ ***Solve***. $42 + (12 - 26) =$ First subtract the numbers in brackets, $12 - 26 = -14$ Then: $42 + (-14) = \;\rightarrow$ change addition into subtraction: $42 - 14 = 28$	
Your Turn!	1) $-(15) + 12 =$	2) $(-2) + (-10) + 18 =$
	3) $(-13) + 7 =$	4) $3 - (-7) + 14 =$
	5) $(-7) + (-8) =$	6) $16 - (-4 + 8) =$
	7) $4 + (-15) + 2 =$	8) $-(22) - (-4) + 8 =$

Name:	Date: ....

Topic	Adding and Subtracting Integers - Answers	
Notes	✓ Integers include: zero, counting numbers, and the negative of the counting numbers. $\{... , -3, -2, -1, 0, 1, 2, 3, ...\}$ ✓ Add a positive integer by moving to the right on the number line. ✓ Add a negative integer by moving to the left on the number line. Subtract an integer by adding its opposite.	
Examples	***Solve.*** $(4) - (-8) =$ Keep the first number and convert the sign of the second number to its opposite. (change subtraction into addition. Then: $(4) + 8 = 12$ ***Solve.*** $42 + (12 - 26) =$ First subtract the numbers in brackets, $12 - 26 = -14$ Then: $42 + (-14) = \;\rightarrow$ change addition into subtraction: $42 - 14 = 28$	
Your Turn!	1) $-(15) + 12 = -3$	2) $(-2) + (-10) + 18 = 6$
	3) $(-13) + 7 = -6$	4) $3 - (-7) + 14 = 24$
	5) $(-7) + (-8) = -15$	6) $16 - (-4 + 8) = 12$
	7) $4 + (-15) + 2 = -9$	8) $(-22) - (-4) + 8 = -10$

Name:	Date: ....

Topic	**Multiplying and Dividing Integers**	
Notes	Use following rules for multiplying and dividing integers: ✓ (negative) × (negative) = positive ✓ (negative) ÷ (negative) = positive ✓ (negative) × (positive) = negative ✓ (negative) ÷ (positive) = negative ✓ (positive) × (positive) = positive ✓ (positive) ÷ (negative) = negative	
Examples	*Solve.* $2 \times (14 - 17) =$ First subtract the numbers in brackets, $14 - 17 = -3 \rightarrow (2) \times (-3) =$ Now use this rule: (positive) × (negative) = negative $(2) \times (-3) = -6$ *Solve.* $(-7) + (-36 \div 4) =$ First divide -36 by 4 , the numbers in brackets, using this rule: (negative) ÷ (positive) = negative Then: $-36 \div 4 = -9$. Now, add -7 and -9: $(-7) + (-9) = -7 - 9 = -16$	
Your Turn!	1) $(-7) \times 6 =$	2) $(-63) \div (-7) =$
	3) $(-11) \times (-3) =$	4) $81 \div (-9) =$
	5) $(15 - 12) \times (-7) =$	6) $(-12) \div (3) =$
	7) $4 \times (-9) =$	8) $(8) \div (-2) =$

Name:	Date: ....

Topic	**Multiplying and Dividing Integers - Answers**	
Notes	Use following rules for multiplying and dividing integers: ✓ (negative) × (negative) = positive ✓ (negative) ÷ (negative) = positive ✓ (negative) × (positive) = negative ✓ (negative) ÷ (positive) = negative ✓ (positive) × (positive) = positive ✓ (positive) ÷ (negative) = negative	
Examples	**Solve.** $2 \times (14 - 17) =$ First subtract the numbers in brackets, $14 - 17 = -3 \rightarrow (2) \times (-3) =$ Now use this rule: (positive) × (negative) = negative $(2) \times (-3) = -6$ **Solve.** $(-7) + (-36 \div 4) =$ First divide -36 by 4 , the numbers in brackets, using this rule: (negative) ÷ (positive) = negative Then: $-36 \div 4 = -9$. Now, add -7 and -9: $(-7) + (-9) = -7 - 9 = -16$	
Your Turn!	1) $(-7) \times 6 = -42$ 3) $(-11) \times (-3) = 33$ 5) $(15 - 12) \times (-7) = -21$ 7) $4 \times (-9) = -36$	2) $(-63) \div (-7) = 9$ 4) $81 \div (-9) = -9$ 6) $(-12) \div (3) = -4$ 8) $(8) \div (-2) = -4$

Name:	Date: ....

Topic	**Order of Operation**
Notes	When there is more than one math operation, use PEMDAS: (to memorize this rule, remember the phrase "Please Excuse My Dear Aunt Sally") ✓ Parentheses ✓ Exponents ✓ Multiplication and Division (from left to right) ✓ Addition and Subtraction (from left to right)
Examples	***Calculate.*** $(18 - 26) \div (2^4 \div 4) =$ First simplify inside parentheses: $(-8) \div (16 \div 4) = (-8) \div (4)$ Then: $(-8) \div (4) = -2$ ***Solve.*** $(-5 \times 7) - (18 - 3^2) =$ First calculate within parentheses: $(-5 \times 7) - (18 - 3^2) = (-35) - (18 - 9)$ Then: $(-35) - (18 - 9) = -35 - 9 = -44$

Your Turn!	1) $(11 \times 4) \div (5 + 6) =$	2) $(30 \div 5) + (17 - 8) =$
	3) $(-9) + (5 \times 6) + 14 =$	4) $(-10 \times 5) \div (2^2 + 1) =$
	5) $[-16(32 \div 2^3)] \div 8 =$	6) $(-7) + (72 \div 3^2) + 12 =$
	7) $[16(32 \div 2^3)] - 4^2 =$	8) $4^3 + (-5 \times 2^5) + 5 =$

Name:	Date: ....

Topic	Order of Operation - Answers
Notes	When there is more than one math operation, use PEMDAS: (to memorize this rule, remember the phrase "Please Excuse My Dear Aunt Sally") ✓ Parentheses ✓ Exponents ✓ Multiplication and Division (from left to right) ✓ Addition and Subtraction (from left to right)
Examples	***Calculate.*** $(18 - 26) \div (2^4 \div 4) =$ First simplify inside parentheses: $(-8) \div (16 \div 4) = (-8) \div (4)$ Then: $(-8) \div (4) = -2$ ***Solve***. $(-5 \times 7) - (18 - 3^2) =$ First calculate within parentheses: $(-5 \times 7) - (18 - 3^2) = (-35) - (18 - 9)$ Then: $(-35) - (18 - 9) = -35 - 9 = -44$

Your Turn!	1) $(11 \times 4) \div (5 + 6) = 4$	2) $(30 \div 5) + (17 - 8) = 15$
	3) $(-9) + (5 \times 6) + 14 =$ 35	4) $(-10 \times 5) \div (2^2 + 1) = -10$
	5) $[-16(32 \div 2^3)] \div 8 =$ -8	6) $(-7) + (72 \div 3^2) + 12 = 13$
	7) $[16(32 \div 2^3)] - 4^2 =$ 48	8) $4^3 + (-5 \times 2^5) + 5 = -91$

Name: ……………………………………	Date: ………………………………………….

Topic	Integers and Absolute Value
Notes	✓ The absolute value of a number is its distance from zero, in either direction, on the number line. For example, the distance of 9 and -9 from zero on number line is 9. ✓ Absolute value is symbolized by vertical bars, as in $\lvert x \rvert$.
Example	*Calculate.* $\lvert 8 - 5 \rvert \times \lvert 12 - 16 \rvert =$ First calculate $\lvert 8 - 5 \rvert$, $\rightarrow \lvert 8 - 5 \rvert = \lvert 3 \rvert$, the absolute value of 3 is 3, $\lvert 3 \rvert = 3$ $8 \times \lvert 12 - 16 \rvert =$ Now calculate $\lvert 12 - 16 \rvert$, $\rightarrow \lvert 12 - 16 \rvert = \lvert -4 \rvert$, the absolute value of -4 is 4, $\lvert -4 \rvert = 4$. Then: $3 \times 4 = 12$

Your Turn!	
1) $11 - \lvert 4 - 13 \rvert =$	2) $14 - \lvert 12 - 19 \rvert - \lvert 9 \rvert =$
3) $\lvert 21 \rvert - \dfrac{\lvert -25 \rvert}{5} =$	4) $\lvert 30 \rvert + \dfrac{\lvert -49 \rvert}{7} =$
5) $\dfrac{\lvert 7 \times -8 \rvert}{4} \times \dfrac{\lvert -12 \rvert}{2} =$	6) $\dfrac{\lvert 10 \times -6 \rvert}{5} \times \lvert -9 \rvert =$
7) $\dfrac{\lvert -20 \rvert}{5} \times \dfrac{\lvert -36 \rvert}{6} =$	8) $\lvert -30 + 6 \rvert \times \dfrac{\lvert -9 \times 4 \rvert}{12} =$

Name:	Date: ....

Topic	Integers and Absolute Value - Answers	
Notes	✓ The absolute value of a number is its distance from zero, in either direction, on the number line. For example, the distance of 9 and -9 from zero on number line is 9. ✓ Absolute value is symbolized by vertical bars, as in $\lvert x \rvert$.	
Example	*Calculate.* $\lvert 8 - 5 \rvert \times \lvert 12 - 16 \rvert =$ First calculate $\lvert 8 - 5 \rvert$, $\rightarrow \lvert 8 - 5 \rvert = \lvert 3 \rvert$, the absolute value of 3 is 3, $\lvert 3 \rvert = 3$ $8 \times \lvert 12 - 16 \rvert =$ Now calculate $\lvert 12 - 16 \rvert$, $\rightarrow \lvert 12 - 16 \rvert = \lvert -4 \rvert$, the absolute value of -4 is 4, $\lvert -4 \rvert = 4$. Then: $3 \times 4 = 12$	
Your Turn!	1) $11 - \lvert 4 - 13 \rvert = 2$	2) $14 - \lvert 12 - 19 \rvert - \lvert 9 \rvert = -2$
	3) $\lvert 21 \rvert - \dfrac{\lvert -25 \rvert}{5} = 16$	4) $\lvert 30 \rvert + \dfrac{\lvert -49 \rvert}{7} = 37$
	5) $\dfrac{\lvert 7 \times -8 \rvert}{4} \times \dfrac{\lvert -12 \rvert}{2} = 84$	6) $\dfrac{\lvert 10 \times -6 \rvert}{5} \times \lvert -9 \rvert = 108$
	7) $\dfrac{\lvert -20 \rvert}{5} \times \dfrac{\lvert -36 \rvert}{6} = 24$	8) $\lvert -30 + 6 \rvert \times \dfrac{\lvert -9 \times 4 \rvert}{12} = 72$

Name:	Date: ....

Topic	**Simplifying Ratios**
Notes	✓ Ratios are used to make comparisons between two numbers. ✓ Ratios can be written as a fraction, using the word "to", or with a colon. ✓ You can calculate equivalent ratios by multiplying or dividing both sides of the ratio by the same number.
Examples	*Simplify.* $18:63 =$ Both numbers 18 and 63 are divisible by $9 \Rightarrow 18 \div 9 = 2,\ 63 \div 9 = 7$, Then: $18:63 = 2:7$ *Simplify.* $\dfrac{25}{45} =$ Both numbers 25 and 45 are divisible by 5, $\Rightarrow 25 \div 5 = 5,\ 45 \div 5 = 9$, Then: $\dfrac{25}{45} = \dfrac{5}{9}$

Your Turn!	1) $\dfrac{4}{32} = -$	2) $\dfrac{25}{80} = -$
	3) $\dfrac{15}{35} = -$	4) $\dfrac{42}{54} = -$
	5) $\dfrac{12}{36} = -$	6) $\dfrac{30}{80} = -$
	7) $\dfrac{18}{24} = -$	8) $\dfrac{60}{108} = -$

Name:	Date: ....

Topic	**Simplifying Ratios - Answers**
Notes	✓ Ratios are used to make comparisons between two numbers. ✓ Ratios can be written as a fraction, using the word "to", or with a colon. ✓ You can calculate equivalent ratios by multiplying or dividing both sides of the ratio by the same number.
Examples	*Simplify.* $18 : 63 =$ Both numbers 18 and 63 are divisible by $9 \Rightarrow 18 \div 9 = 2, 63 \div 9 = 7$, Then: $18 : 63 = 2 : 7$ *Simplify.* $\frac{25}{45} =$ Both numbers 25 and 45 are divisible by 5, $\Rightarrow 25 \div 5 = 5, 45 \div 5 = 9$, Then: $\frac{25}{45} = \frac{5}{9}$
Your Turn!	1) $\frac{4}{32} = \frac{1}{8}$ 2) $\frac{25}{80} = \frac{5}{16}$ 3) $\frac{15}{35} = \frac{3}{7}$ 4) $\frac{42}{54} = \frac{7}{9}$ 5) $\frac{12}{36} = \frac{1}{3}$ 6) $\frac{30}{80} = \frac{3}{8}$ 7) 8) $\frac{18}{24} = \frac{3}{4}$ 9) $\frac{60}{108} = \frac{5}{9}$

Name:	Date: ....

Topic	**Proportional Ratios**
Notes	✓ Two ratios are proportional if they represent the same relationship. ✓ A proportion means that two ratios are equal. It can be written in two ways: $$\frac{a}{b} = \frac{c}{d} \qquad\qquad a : b = c : d$$
Example	***Solve this proportion for*** x. $\dfrac{5}{8} = \dfrac{35}{x}$ Use cross multiplication: $\dfrac{5}{8} = \dfrac{35}{x} \Rightarrow 5 \times x = 8 \times 35 \Rightarrow 5x = 280$ Divide to find x: $\quad x = \dfrac{280}{5} \Rightarrow x = 56$
Your Turn!	1) $\dfrac{1}{9} = \dfrac{8}{x} \Rightarrow x = $ ____ 2) $\dfrac{5}{8} = \dfrac{25}{x} \Rightarrow x = $ ____ 3) $\dfrac{3}{11} = \dfrac{6}{x} \Rightarrow x = $ ____ 4) $\dfrac{12}{20} = \dfrac{x}{200} \Rightarrow x = $ ____ 5) $\dfrac{9}{12} = \dfrac{27}{x} \Rightarrow x = $ ____ 6) $\dfrac{14}{16} = \dfrac{x}{80} \Rightarrow x = $ ____ 7) $\dfrac{7}{15} = \dfrac{49}{x} \Rightarrow x = $ ____ 8) $\dfrac{8}{19} = \dfrac{32}{x} \Rightarrow x = $ ____

Name:	Date: ....

Topic	**Proportional Ratios - Answers**
Notes	✓ Two ratios are proportional if they represent the same relationship. ✓ A proportion means that two ratios are equal. It can be written in two ways: $\dfrac{a}{b} = \dfrac{c}{d}$ $\qquad a : b = c : d$
Example	***Solve this proportion for*** $x. \dfrac{5}{8} = \dfrac{35}{x}$ Use cross multiplication: $\dfrac{5}{8} = \dfrac{35}{x} \Rightarrow 5 \times x = 8 \times 35 \Rightarrow 5x = 280$ Divide to find x: $\quad x = \dfrac{280}{5} \Rightarrow x = 56$

Your Turn!	1) $\dfrac{1}{9} = \dfrac{8}{x} \Rightarrow x = 72$	2) $\dfrac{5}{8} = \dfrac{25}{x} \Rightarrow x = 40$
	3) $\dfrac{3}{11} = \dfrac{6}{x} \Rightarrow x = 22$	4) $\dfrac{12}{20} = \dfrac{x}{200} \Rightarrow x = 120$
	5) $\dfrac{9}{12} = \dfrac{27}{x} \Rightarrow x = 36$	6) $\dfrac{14}{16} = \dfrac{x}{80} \Rightarrow x = 70$
	7) $\dfrac{7}{15} = \dfrac{49}{x} \Rightarrow x = 105$	8) $\dfrac{8}{19} = \dfrac{32}{x} \Rightarrow x = 76$

Name:	Date: ....

Topic	Create Proportion
Notes	✓ To create a proportion, simply find (or create) two equal fractions. ✓ Use cross products to solve proportions or to test whether two ratios are equal and form a proportion. $\frac{a}{b} = \frac{c}{d} \Rightarrow a \times d = c \times b$
Example	***State if this pair of ratios form a proportion.*** $\frac{2}{3}$ *and* $\frac{12}{30}$ Use cross multiplication: $\frac{2}{3} = \frac{12}{30} \rightarrow 2 \times 30 = 12 \times 3 \rightarrow 60 = 36$, which is not correct. Therefore, this pair of ratios doesn't form a proportion.

Your Turn!	***State if each pair of ratios form a proportion.***

1) $\frac{4}{8}$ *and* $\frac{24}{48}$	2) $\frac{5}{15}$ *and* $\frac{10}{20}$
3) $\frac{3}{11}$ *and* $\frac{9}{33}$	4) $\frac{7}{10}$ *and* $\frac{14}{20}$
5) $\frac{7}{9}$ *and* $\frac{48}{81}$	6) $\frac{6}{8}$ *and* $\frac{12}{14}$
7) $\frac{2}{10}$ *and* $\frac{6}{30}$	8) $\frac{9}{12}$ *and* $\frac{18}{24}$

9) Solve.

Five pencils costs $0.65. How many pencils can you buy for $2.60? _____

| Name: .... | Date: .... |

Topic	Create Proportion
Notes	✓ To create a proportion, simply find (or create) two equal fractions. ✓ Use cross products to solve proportions or to test whether two ratios are equal and form a proportion. $\frac{a}{b} = \frac{c}{d} \Rightarrow a \times d = c \times b$
Example	***State if this pair of ratios form a proportion.*** $\frac{2}{3} \, and \, \frac{12}{30}$ Use cross multiplication: $\frac{2}{3} = \frac{12}{30} \rightarrow 2 \times 30 = 12 \times 3 \rightarrow 60 = 36$, which is not correct. Therefore, this pair of ratios doesn't form a proportion.

	State if each pair of ratios form a proportion.
Your Turn!	1) $\frac{4}{8} \, and \, \frac{24}{48}, Yes$ $\quad$ 2) $\frac{5}{15} \, and \, \frac{10}{20}, No$
	3) $\frac{3}{11} \, and \, \frac{9}{33}, Yes$ $\quad$ 4) $\frac{7}{10} \, and \, \frac{14}{20}, Yes$
	5) $\frac{7}{9} \, and \, \frac{48}{81}, No$ $\quad$ 6) $\frac{6}{8} \, and \, \frac{12}{14}, No$
	7) $\frac{2}{10} \, and \, \frac{6}{30}, Yes$ $\quad$ 8) $\frac{9}{12} \, and \, \frac{18}{24}, Yes$
	9) Solve. Five pencils costs $0.65. How many pencils can you buy for $2.60? **20 pencils**

Name: ....   **Date:** ....

Topic	**Similarity and Ratios**
Notes	✓ Two figures are similar if they have the same shape. ✓ Two or more figures are similar if the corresponding angles are equal, and the corresponding sides are in proportion.

Example	*Following triangles are similar. What is the value of unknown side?* **Solution:** Find the corresponding sides and write a proportion: $\frac{4}{12} = \frac{x}{9}$. Now, use cross product to solve for x: $\frac{4}{12} = \frac{x}{9} \rightarrow 4 \times 9 = 12 \times x \rightarrow 36 = 12x$. Divide both sides by 12. Then: $5x = 40 \rightarrow \frac{36}{12} = \frac{12x}{12} \rightarrow x = 3$. The missing side is 3.

Your Turn!

1)

2)

3)

4)

5)

6)

Name:	Date: ....

Topic	**Similarity and Ratios - Answers**
Notes	✓ Two figures are similar if they have the same shape. ✓ Two or more figures are similar if the corresponding angles are equal, and the corresponding sides are in proportion.
Example	*Following triangles are similar. What is the value of unknown side?* **Solution:** Find the corresponding sides and write a proportion: $\frac{4}{12} = \frac{x}{9}$. Now, use cross product to solve for x: $\frac{4}{12} = \frac{x}{9} \rightarrow 4 \times 9 = 12 \times x \rightarrow 36 = 12x$. Divide both sides by 12. Then: $5x = 40 \rightarrow \frac{36}{12} = \frac{12x}{12} \rightarrow x = 3$. The missing side is 3.

Your Turn!

1) 24

2) 11

3) 4

4) 8

5) 10

6) 9

Name:	Date: ....

Topic	Percent Problems

Notes	✓ In each percent problem, we are looking for the base, or part or the percent.
	✓ Use the following equations to find each missing section.
	    ○ Base = Part ÷ Percent
	    ○ Part = Percent × Base
	    ○ Percent = Part ÷ Base

Examples	**18 *is what percent of* 30?** In this problem, we are looking for the percent. Use the following equation: $$Percent = Part \div Base \rightarrow Percent = 18 \div 30 = 0.6 = 60\%$$ **40 *is* 20% *of what number?*** Use the following formula: $Base = Part \div Percent \rightarrow Base = 40 \div 0.20 = 200$ 40 is 20% of 200.

Your Turn!	1) What is 25 percent of 800?	2) 26 is what percent of 200?
	3) 60 is 5 percent of what number?	4) 48 is what percent of 300?
	5) 84 is 28 percent of what number?	6) 63 is what percent of 700?
	7) 96 is 24 percent of what number?	8) 40 is what percent of 800?

Name:	**Date:** ....

Topic	**Percent Problems – Answers**

Notes	✓ In each percent problem, we are looking for the base, or part or the percent.
	✓ Use the following equations to find each missing section.
	     ○ Base = Part ÷ Percent
	     ○ Part = Percent × Base
	     ○ Percent = Part ÷ Base

Topic	
Examples	**18 *is what percent of* 30?** In this problem, we are looking for the percent. Use the following equation: $$Percent = Part \div Base \rightarrow Percent = 18 \div 30 = 0.6 = 60\%$$ **40 *is* 20% *of what number?*** Use the following formula: $Base = Part \div Percent \rightarrow Base = 40 \div 0.20 = 200$ 40 is 20% of 200.

Your Turn!	1) What is 25 percent of 800? 200	2) 26 is what percent of 200? 13%
	3) 60 is 5 percent of what number? 1,200	4) 48 is what percent of 300? 16%
	5) 84 is 28 percent of what number? 300	6) 63 is what percent of 700? 9%
	7) 96 is 24 percent of what number? 400	8) 40 is what percent of 800? 5%

Name:	Date: ....

Topic	**Percent of Increase and Decrease**
Notes	✓ Percent of change (increase or decrease) is a mathematical concept that represents the degree of change over time. ✓ To find the percentage of increase or decrease: 1- New Number − Original Number 2- The result ÷ Original Number × 100 Or use this formula: Percent of change = $\frac{new\ number - original\ number}{original\ number} \times 100$
Example	The price of a printer increases from \$40 to \$50. What is the percent increase? **Solution:** Percent of change = $\frac{new\ number - original\ number}{original\ number} \times 100 = \frac{50-40}{40} \times 100 = 25$ The percentage increase is 25. It means that the price of the printer increased 25%.
Your Turn!	1) In a class, the number of students has been increased from 32 to 36. What is the percentage increase? _____ % 2) The price of gasoline rose from \$4.50 to \$5.40 in one month. By what percent did the gas price rise? _____ % 3) A shirt was originally priced at \$65.00. It went on sale for \$52.00. What was the percent that the shirt was discounted? _____ % 4) Jason got a raise, and his hourly wage increased from \$40 to \$52. What is the percent increase? _____ %

Name:	Date: ....

Topic	**Percent of Increase and Decrease - Answers**
Notes	✓ Percent of change (increase or decrease) is a mathematical concept that represents the degree of change over time. ✓ To find the percentage of increase or decrease: 1- New Number – Original Number 2- The result ÷ Original Number × 100 Or use this formula: Percent of change = $\frac{new\ number - original\ number}{original\ number} \times 100$
Example	The price of a printer increases from \$40 to \$50. What is the percent increase? **Solution:** Percent of change = $\frac{new\ number - original\ number}{original\ number} \times 100 = \frac{50-40}{40} \times 100 = 25$ The percentage increase is 25. It means that the price of the printer increased 25%.
Your Turn!	1) In a class, the number of students has been increased from 32 to 36. What is the percentage increase? 12.5% 2) The price of gasoline rose from \$4.50 to \$5.40 in one month. By what percent did the gas price rise? 20% 3) A shirt was originally priced at \$65.00. It went on sale for \$52.00. What was the percent that the shirt was discounted? 20% 4) Jason got a raise, and his hourly wage increased from \$40 to \$52. What is the percent increase? 30%

Name:	Date: ....

Topic	**Discount, Tax and Tip**	
Notes	✓ Discount = Multiply the regular price by the rate of discount ✓ Selling price = original price – discount ✓ To find tax, multiply the tax rate to the taxable amount (income, property value, etc.) ✓ To find tip, multiply the rate to the selling price.	
Example	The original price of a table is $300 and the tax rate is 6%. What is the final price of the table? **Solution:** First find the tax amount. To find tax: Multiply the tax rate to the taxable amount. Tax rate is 6% or 0.06. Then: $0.06 \times 300 = 18$. The tax amount is $18. Final price is: $300 + $18 = $318	
Your Turn!	1) Original price of a chair: $300 Tax: 15%, Selling price: _____	2) Original price of a computer: $750 Discount: 20%, Selling price: _____
	3) Original price of a printer: $250 Tax: 10%, Selling price: _____	4) Original price of a sofa: $620 Discount: 25%, Selling price: _____
	5) Original price of a mattress: $800 Tax: 12%, Selling price: _____	6) Original price of a book: $150 Discount: 60%, Selling price: _____
	7) Restaurant bill: $35.00 Tip: 20%, Final amount: _____	8) Restaurant bill: $60.00 Tip: 25%, Final amount: _____

Name:	Date: ....

Topic	**Discount, Tax and Tip - Answers**
Notes	✓ Discount = Multiply the regular price by the rate of discount ✓ Selling price = original price – discount ✓ To find tax, multiply the tax rate to the taxable amount (income, property value, etc.) ✓ To find tip, multiply the rate to the selling price.
Example	**The original price of a table is $300 and the tax rate is 6%. What is the final price of the table?** **Solution:** First find the tax amount. To find tax: Multiply the tax rate to the taxable amount. Tax rate is 6% or 0.06. Then: $0.06 \times 300 = 18$. The tax amount is $18. Final price is: $300 + \$18 = \$318$

Your Turn!	1) Original price of a chair: $300 Tax: 15%, Selling price: $345	2) Original price of a computer: $750 Discount: 20%, Selling price: $600
	3) Original price of a printer: $250 Tax: 10%, Selling price: $275	4) Original price of a sofa: $620 Discount: 25%, Selling price: $465
	5) Original price of a mattress: $800 Tax: 12%, Selling price: $896	6) Original price of a book: $150 Discount: 60%, Selling price: $60
	7) Restaurant bill: $35.00 Tip: 20%, Final amount: $42	8) Restaurant bill: $60.00 Tip: 25%, Final amount: $75

Name:	Date: ....

Topic	**Simple Interest**	
Notes	✓ Simple Interest: The charge for borrowing money or the return for lending it. To solve a simple interest problem, use this formula: Interest = principal x rate x time $\Rightarrow$ $I = p \times r \times t$	

Example	***Find simple interest for*** $3,000$ ***investment at*** 5% ***for 4 years.***
	  Solution: Use Interest formula: $I = prt$ ($P = \$3,000$, r = 5\% = 0.05 and $t = 4$)
	  Then: $I = 3,000 \times 0.05 \times 4 = \$600$	

Your Turn!	1) $250 at 4% for 3 years.
	     Simple interest: $_____
		2) $3,300 at 5% for 6 years.
		     Simple interest: $_____

	3) $720 at 2% for 5 years.
	     Simple interest: $_____
		4) $2,200 at 8% for 4 years.
		     Simple interest: $_____

	5) $1,800 at 3% for 2 years.
	     Simple interest: $_____
		6) $530 at 4% for 5 years.
		     Simple interest: $_____

	7) $7,000 at 5% for 3 months.
	     Simple interest: $_____
		8) $880 at 5% for 9 months.
		     Simple interest: $_____

Name: ....   **Date:** ....

Topic	**Simple Interest - Answers**
Notes	✓ Simple Interest: The charge for borrowing money or the return for lending it. To solve a simple interest problem, use this formula: Interest = principal x rate x time $\Rightarrow I = p \times r \times t$
Example	**Find simple interest for** $3,000 **investment at** 5% **for 4 years.** **Solution:** Use Interest formula: $I = prt$ ($P = \$3,000$, r $= 5\% = 0.05$ and $t = 4$) Then: $I = 3,000 \times 0.05 \times 4 = \$600$

Your Turn!		
	1) $250 at 4% for 3 years. Simple interest: $30	2) $3,300 at 5% for 6 years. Simple interest: $990
	3) $720 at 2% for 5 years. Simple interest: $72	4) $2,200 at 8% for 4 years. Simple interest: $704
	5) $1,800 at 3% for 2 years. Simple interest: $108	6) $530 at 4% for 5 years. Simple interest: $106
	7) $7,000 at 5% for 3 months. Simple interest: $87.50	8) $880 at 5% for 9 months. Simple interest: $33

| Name: .... | Date: .... |

Topic	**Simplifying Variable Expressions**
Notes	✓ In algebra, a variable is a letter used to stand for a number. The most common letters are: $x, y, z, a, b, c, m, and\ n$. ✓ Algebraic expression is an expression contains integers, variables, and the math operations such as addition, subtraction, multiplication, division, etc. ✓ In an expression, we can combine "like" terms. (values with same variable and same power)
Example	*Simplify this expression*. $(6x + 8x + 9) =?$ Combine like terms. Then: $(6x + 8x + 4) = 14x + 9$ **(remember you cannot combine variables and numbers).**

Your Turn!	1) $5x + 2 - 2x =$	2) $4 + 7x + 3x =$
	3) $8x + 3 - 3x =$	4) $-2 - x^2 - 6x^2 =$
	5) $3 + 10x^2 + 2 =$	6) $8x^2 + 6x + 7x^2 =$
	7) $5x^2 - 12x^2 + 8x =$	8) $2x^2 - 2x - x + 5x^2 =$
	9) $4x - (12 - 30x) =$	10) $10x - (80x - 48) =$

Name:	Date: ....

Topic	**Simplifying Variable Expressions - Answers**	
Notes	✓ In algebra, a variable is a letter used to stand for a number. The most common letters are: $x, y, z, a, b, c, m, and\ n$. ✓ Algebraic expression is an expression contains integers, variables, and the math operations such as addition, subtraction, multiplication, division, etc. ✓ In an expression, we can combine "like" terms. (values with same variable and same power)	
Example	***Simplify this expression.*** $(6x + 8x + 9) =?$ Combine like terms. Then: $(6x + 8x + 4) = 14x + 9$ ***(remember you cannot combine variables and numbers).***	
Your Turn!	1) $5x + 2 - 2x =$ $\qquad 3x + 2$	2) $4 + 7x + 3x =$ $\qquad 10x + 4$
	3) $8x + 3 - 3x =$ $\qquad 5x + 3$	4) $-2 - x^2 - 6x^2 =$ $\qquad -7x^2 - 2$
	5) $3 + 10x^2 + 2 =$ $\qquad 10x^2 + 5$	6) $8x^2 + 6x + 7x^2 =$ $\qquad 15x^2 + 6x$
	7) $5x^2 - 12x^2 + 8x =$ $\qquad -7x^2 + 8x$	8) $2x^2 - 2x - x + 5x^2 =$ $\qquad 72x^2 - 3x$
	9) $4x - (12 - 30x) =$ $\qquad 34x - 12$	10) $\quad 10x - (80x - 48) =$ $\qquad -70x - 48$

Name:	Date: ....

Topic	Simplifying Polynomial Expressions	
Notes	✓ In mathematics, a polynomial is an expression consisting of variables and coefficients that involves only the operations of addition, subtraction, multiplication, and non–negative integer exponents of variables. $$P(x) = a_n x^n + a_{n-1} x^{n-1} + \dots + a_2 x^2 + a_1 x + a_0$$	
Example	***Simplify this expression.*** $(2x^2 - x^4) - (4x^4 - x^2) =$ First use distributive property: $\rightarrow$ multiply $(-)$ into $(4x^4 - x^2)$ $(2x^2 - x^4) - (4x^4 - x^2) = 2x^2 - x^4 - 4x^4 + x^2$ Then combine "like" terms: $2x^2 - x^4 - 4x^4 + x^2 = 3x^2 - 5x^4$ And write in standard form: $3x^2 - 5x^4 = -5x^4 + 3x^2$	
Your Turn!	1) $(2x^3 + 5x^2) - (12x + 2x^2) =$	2) $(2x^5 + 2x^3) - (7x^3 + 6x^2) =$
	3) $(12x^4 + 4x^2) - (2x^2 - 6x^4) =$	4) $14x - 3x^2 - 2(6x^2 + 6x^3) =$
	5) $(5x^3 - 3) + 5(2x^2 - 3x^3) =$	6) $(4x^3 - 2x) - 2(4x^3 - 2x^4) =$
	7) $2(4x - 3x^3) - 3(3x^3 + 4x^2) =$	8) $(2x^2 - 2x) - (2x^3 + 5x^2) =$

Name:	Date: ....

Topic	**Simplifying Polynomial Expressions - Answers**
Notes	✓ In mathematics, a polynomial is an expression consisting of variables and coefficients that involves only the operations of addition, subtraction, multiplication, and non–negative integer exponents of variables. $$P(x) = a_n x^n + a_{n-1} x^{n-1} + \ldots + a_2 x^2 + a_1 x + a_0$$
Example	**Simplify this expression.** $(2x^2 - x^4) - (4x^4 - x^2) =$ First use distributive property: → multiply $(-)$ into $(4x^4 - x^2)$ $(2x^2 - x^4) - (4x^4 - x^2) = 2x^2 - x^4 - 4x^4 + x^2$ Then combine "like" terms: $2x^2 - x^4 - 4x^4 + x^2 = 3x^2 - 5x^4$ And write in standard form: $3x^2 - 5x^4 = -5x^4 + 3x^2$

Your Turn!	1) $(2x^3 + 5x^2) - (12x + 2x^2) =$ $2x^3 + 3x^2 - 12x$	2) $(2x^5 + 2x^3) - (7x^3 + 6x^2) =$ $2x^5 - 5x^3 - 6x^2$
	3) $(12x^4 + 4x^2) - (2x^2 - 6x^4) =$ $18x^4 + 2x^2$	4) $14x - 3x^2 - 2(6x^2 + 6x^3) =$ $-12x^3 - 15x^2 + 14x$
	5) $(5x^3 - 3) + 5(2x^2 - 3x^3) =$ $-10x^3 + 10x^2 - 3$	6) $(4x^3 - 2x) - 2(4x^3 - 2x^4) =$ $4x^4 - 4x^3 - 2$
	7) $2(4x - 3x^3) - 3(3x^3 + 4x^2) =$ $-15x^3 - 12x^2 + 8x$	8) $(2x^2 - 2x) - (2x^3 + 5x^2) =$ $-2x^3 - 3x^2 - 2x$

Name:	Date: ....

Topic	**Evaluating One Variable**
Notes	✓ To evaluate one variable expression, find the variable and substitute a number for that variable. ✓ Perform the arithmetic operations.
Example	**Find the value of this expression for** $x = -3$. $-3x - 13$ **Solution:** Substitute -3 for x, then: $-3x - 13 = -3(-3) - 13 = 9 - 13 = -4$
Your Turn!	1) $x = -3 \Rightarrow 3x + 8 =$ _____ 2) $x = 4 \Rightarrow 4(2x + 6) =$ _____ 3) $x = -1 \Rightarrow 6x + 4 =$ _____ 4) $x = 7 \Rightarrow 6(5x + 3) =$ _____ 5) $x = 4 \Rightarrow 5(3x + 2) =$ ___ 6) $x = 6 \Rightarrow 3(2x + 4) =$ _____ 7) $x = 3 \Rightarrow 7(3x + 1) =$ ___ 8) $x = 8 \Rightarrow 3(3x + 7) =$ _____ 9) $x = 9 \Rightarrow 2(x + 9) =$ _____ 10) $x = 7 \Rightarrow 2(4x + 5) =$ _____

Name:	Date: ....

Topic	**Evaluating One Variable - Answers**
Notes	✓ To evaluate one variable expression, find the variable and substitute a number for that variable. ✓ Perform the arithmetic operations.
Example	*Find the value of this expression for* $x = -3$. $\quad -3x - 13$ **Solution:** Substitute -3 for x, then: $-3x - 13 = -3(-3) - 13 = 9 - 13 = -4$

Your Turn!	1) $x = -3 \Rightarrow 3x + 8 = -1$	2) $x = 4 \Rightarrow 4(2x + 6) = 56$
	3) $x = -1 \Rightarrow 6x + 4 = -2$	4) $x = 7 \Rightarrow 6(5x + 3) = 228$
	5) $x = 4 \Rightarrow 5(3x + 2) = 70$	6) $x = 6 \Rightarrow 3(2x + 4) = 48$
	7) $x = 3 \Rightarrow 7(3x + 1) = 70$	8) $x = 8 \Rightarrow 3(3x + 7) = 93$
	9) $x = 9 \Rightarrow 2(x + 9) = 36$	10) $x = 7 \Rightarrow 2(4x + 5) = 66$

Name:	Date: ....

Topic	**Evaluating Two Variables**
Notes	✓ To evaluate an algebraic expression, substitute a number for each variable. ✓ Perform the arithmetic operations to find the value of the expression.
Example	*Evaluate this expression for* $a = 4$ *and* $b = -2$. $\quad 5a - 6b$ **Solution:** Substitute 4 for a, and -2 for b, then: $$5a - 6b = 5(4) - 6(-2) = 20 + 12 = 32$$

Your Turn!	1) $-4a + 6b$, $a = 4$, $b = 3$ _____	2) $5x + 3y$, $x = 2$, $y = -1$ _____
	3) $-5a + 3b$, $a = 2$, $b = -2$ _____	4) $3x - 4y$, $x = 6$, $y = 2$ _____
	5) $2z + 14 + 6k$, $z = 5$, $\qquad k = 3$ _____	6) $7a - (9 - 3b)$, $a = 1$, $\qquad b = 1$ _____
	7) $-6a + 3b$, $a = 4$, $b = 3$ _____	8) $-2a + b$, $a = 6$, $b = 9$ _____
	9) $8x + 2y$, $x = 4$, $y = 5$ _____	10) $z + 4 + 2k$, $z = 7$, $k = 4$ _____

Name:	Date: ....

Topic	**Evaluating Two Variables - Answers**
Notes	✓ To evaluate an algebraic expression, substitute a number for each variable. ✓ Perform the arithmetic operations to find the value of the expression.
Example	*Evaluate this expression for* $a = 4$ *and* $b = -2$. $5a - 6b$ **Solution:** Substitute 4 for a, and -2 for b , then: $$5a - 6b = 5(4) - 6(-2) = 20 + 12 = 32$$

Your Turn!	1) $-4a + 6b$, $a = 4$, $b = 3$ 　2	2) $5x + 3y$, $x = 2$, $y = -1$ 　7
	3) $-5a + 3b$, $a = 2$, $b = -2$ 　-16	4) $3x - 4y$, $x = 6$, $y = 2$ 　10
	5) $2z + 14 + 6k$, $z = 5$, 　　　　　$k = 3$ 　42	6) $7a - (9 - 3b)$, $a = 1$, 　　　　　$b = 1$ 　1
	7) $-6a + 3b$, $a = 4$, $b = 3$ 　-15	8) $-2a + b$, $a = 6$, $b = 9$ 　-3
	9) $8x + 2y$, $x = 4$, $y = 5$ 　42	10) $z + 4 + 2k$, $z = 7$, $k = 4$ 　19

Name:	Date: ....

Topic	**The Distributive Property**
Notes	✓ The distributive property (or the distributive property of multiplication over addition and subtraction) simplifies and solves expressions in the form of: $a(b + c)$ or $a(b - c)$ ✓ Distributive Property rule: $$a(b + c) = ab + ac$$
Example	***Simply.*** $(5)(2x - 8)$ **Solution:** Use Distributive Property rule: $a(b + c) = ab + ac$ $$(5)(2x - 8) = (5 \times 2x) + (5) \times (-8) = 10x - 40$$

Your Turn!		
	1) $(-2)(4 - 3x) =$	2) $(6 - 3x)(-7)$
	3) $6\,(5 - 9x) =$	4) $10(3 - 5x) =$
	5) $5(6 - 5x) =$	6) $(-2)(-5x + 3) =$
	7) $(8 - 9x)(5) =$	8) $(-16x + 15)(-3) =$
	9) $(-2x + 7)(3) =$	10) $(-18x + 25)(-2) =$

Name:	Date: ....

Topic	**The Distributive Property - Answers**	
Notes	✓ The distributive property (or the distributive property of multiplication over addition and subtraction) simplifies and solves expressions in the form of: $a(b + c)$ or $a(b - c)$ ✓ Distributive Property rule: $$a(b + c) = ab + ac$$	
Example	***Simply.*** $(5)(2x - 8)$ **Solution:** Use Distributive Property rule: $a(b + c) = ab + ac$ $$(5)(2x - 8) = (5 \times 2x) + (5) \times (-8) = 10x - 40$$	
Your Turn!	1) $(-2)(4 - 3x) = 6x - 8$	2) $(6 - 3x)(-7) = 21x - 42$
	3) $6(5 - 9x) = -54x + 30$	4) $10(3 - 5x) = -50x + 30$
	5) $5(6 - 5x) = -25x + 30$	6) $(-2)(-5x + 3) = 10x - 6$
	7) $(8 - 9x)(5) = -45x + 40$	8) $(-16x + 15)(-3) =$ $48x - 45$
	9) $(-2x + 7)(3) = -6x + 21$	10) $(-18x + 25)(-2) =$ $36x - 50$

Name:	Date: ....

Topic	**One–Step Equations**

Notes	✓ You only need to perform one Math operation in order to solve the one-step equations.
	✓ To solve one-step equation, find the inverse (opposite) operation is being performed.
	✓ The inverse operations are:
	   - Addition and subtraction
	   - Multiplication and division

Example	***Solve this equation.*** $\;x + 42 = 60 \Rightarrow x = ?$ Here, the operation is addition and its inverse operation is subtraction. To solve this equation, subtract 42 from both sides of the *equation:* $x + 42 - 42 = 60 - 42$ Then simplify: $x + 42 - 42 = 60 - 42 \Rightarrow x = 18$
Your Turn!	1) $x - 15 = 36 \Rightarrow x =$ ____ 2) $18 = 13 + x \Rightarrow x =$ ____ 3) $x - 22 = 54 \Rightarrow x =$ ____ 4) $x + 14 = 24 \Rightarrow x =$ ____ 5) $4x = 24 \Rightarrow x =$ ____ 6) $\frac{x}{6} = -3 \Rightarrow x =$ ____ 7) $99 = 11x \Rightarrow x =$ ____ 8) $\frac{x}{12} = 6 \Rightarrow x =$ ____

Name:	Date: ....

Topic	One–Step Equations - Answers	

Notes	✓ You only need to perform one Math operation in order to solve the one-step equations.
	 ✓ To solve one-step equation, find the inverse (opposite) operation is being performed.
	 ✓ The inverse operations are:
	     - Addition and subtraction
	     - Multiplication and division	

Example	***Solve this equation.*** $x + 42 = 60 \Rightarrow x = ?$ Here, the operation is addition and its inverse operation is subtraction. To solve this equation, subtract 42 from both sides of the *equation*: $x + 42 - 42 = 60 - 42$ Then simplify: $x + 42 - 42 = 60 - 42 \Rightarrow x = 18$	
Your Turn!	1) $x - 15 = 36 \Rightarrow x = 51$	2) $18 = 13 + x \Rightarrow x = 5$
	3) $x - 22 = 54 \Rightarrow x = 76$	4) $x + 14 = 24 \Rightarrow x = 10$
	5) $4x = 24 \Rightarrow x = 6$	6) $\frac{x}{6} = -3 \Rightarrow x = -18$
	7) $99 = 11x \Rightarrow x = 9$	8) $\frac{x}{12} = 6 \Rightarrow x = 72$

Name:	**Date:** ....

Topic	**Multi –Step Equations - Answers**
Notes	✓ Combine "like" terms on one side. ✓ Bring variables to one side by adding or subtracting. ✓ Simplify using the inverse of addition or subtraction. ✓ Simplify further by using the inverse of multiplication or division. ✓ Check your solution by plugging the value of the variable into the original equation.
Example	***Solve this equation for*** x. $\quad 2x - 3 = 13$ **Solution:** The inverse of subtraction is addition. Add 3 to both sides of the equation. Then: $2x - 3 = 13 \Rightarrow 2x - 3 = 13 + 3$ $\Rightarrow 2x = 16$. Now, divide both sides by 2, then: $\frac{2x}{2} = \frac{16}{2} \Rightarrow x = 8$ Now, check the solution: $x = 8 \Rightarrow 2x - 3 = 13 \Rightarrow 2(8) - 3 = 13 \Rightarrow 16 - 3 = 13 \qquad$ The answer $x = 8$ is correct.
Your Turn!	1) $4x - 12 = 8 \Rightarrow x =$ 2) $12 - 3x = -6 + 3x \Rightarrow x =$ 3) $3(4 - 2x) = 24 \Rightarrow x =$ 4) $15 + 5x = -7 - 6x \Rightarrow x =$ 5) $-2(5 + x) = 2 \Rightarrow x =$ 6) $12 - 2x = -3 - 5x \Rightarrow x =$ 7) $14 = -(x - 9) \Rightarrow x =$ 8) $11 - 4x = -4 - 3x \Rightarrow x =$

Name:	Date: ....

Topic	**Multi –Step Equations - Answers**
Notes	✓ Combine "like" terms on one side. ✓ Bring variables to one side by adding or subtracting. ✓ Simplify using the inverse of addition or subtraction. ✓ Simplify further by using the inverse of multiplication or division. ✓ Check your solution by plugging the value of the variable into the original equation.
Example	*Solve this equation for* x. $\quad 2x - 3 = 13$ **Solution:** The inverse of subtraction is addition. Add 3 to both sides of the equation. Then: $2x - 3 = 13 \Rightarrow 2x - 3 = 13 + 3$ $\Rightarrow 2x = 16$. Now, divide both sides by 2, then: $\frac{2x}{2} = \frac{16}{2} \Rightarrow x = 8$ Now, check the solution: $x = 8 \Rightarrow 2x - 3 = 13 \Rightarrow 2(8) - 3 = 13 \Rightarrow 16 - 3 = 13 \qquad$ The answer $x = 8$ is correct.

Your Turn!	1) $4x - 12 = 8 \Rightarrow x = 5$	2) $12 - 3x = -6 + 3x \Rightarrow x = 3$
	3) $3(4 - 2x) = 24 \Rightarrow x = -2$	4) $15 + 5x = -7 - 6x \Rightarrow x = -2$
	5) $-2(5 + x) = 2 \Rightarrow x = -6$	6) $12 - 2x = -3 - 5x \Rightarrow x = -5$
	7) $14 = -(x - 9) \Rightarrow x = -5$	8) $11 - 4x = -4 - 3x \Rightarrow x = 15$

Name:		Date: ....

Topic	**System of Equations**	
Notes	✓ A system of equations contains two equations and two variables. For example, consider the system of equations: $x - 2y = -2$, $x + 2y = 10$ ✓ The easiest way to solve a system of equation is using the elimination method. The elimination method uses the addition property of equality. You can add the same value to each side of an equation. ✓ For the first equation above, you can add $x + 2y$ to the left side and 10 to the right side of the first equation: $x - 2y + (x + 2y) = -2 + 10$. Now, if you simplify, you get: $x - 2y + (x + 2y) = -2 + 10 \rightarrow 2x = 8 \rightarrow x = 4$. Now, substitute 4 for the x in the first equation: $4 - 2y = -2$. By solving this equation, $y = 3$	
Example	What is the value of x and y in this system of equations? $\begin{cases} 3x - y = 7 \\ -x + 4y = 5 \end{cases}$ **Solution:** Solving System of Equations by Elimination: $\dfrac{3x - y = 7}{-x + 4y = 5}$ Multiply the second equation by 3, then add it to the first equation. $\dfrac{3x - y = 7}{3(-x + 4y = 5)} \Rightarrow \dfrac{3x - y = 7}{-3x + 12y = 15)} \Rightarrow 11y = 22 \Rightarrow y = 2$. Now, substitute 2 for y in the first equation and solve for x. $3x - (2) = 7 \Rightarrow 3x = 9 \Rightarrow x = 3$	
Your Turn!	1) $-4x + 4y = 8$ $-4x + 2y = 6$ $x = $ ___ $y = $ ___	2) $-5x + y = -3$ $3x - 8y = 24$ $x = $ ___ $y = $ ___
	3) $y = -2$ $4x - 3y = 8$ $x = $ ___ $y = $ ___	4) $y = -3x + 5$ $5x - 4y = -3$ $x = $ ___ $y = $ ___
	5) $20x - 18y = -26$ $-10x + 6y = 22$ $x = $ ___ $y = $ ___	6) $-9x - 12y = 15$ $2x - 6y = 14$ $x = $ ___ $y = $ ___

Name:	Date: ....

Topic	System of Equations- Answers
Notes	✓ A system of equations contains two equations and two variables. For example, consider the system of equations: $x - 2y = -2, x + 2y = 10$ ✓ The easiest way to solve a system of equation is using the elimination method. The elimination method uses the addition property of equality. You can add the same value to each side of an equation. ✓ For the first equation above, you can add $x + 2y$ to the left side and 10 to the right side of the first equation: $x - 2y + (x + 2y) = -2 + 10$. Now, if you simplify, you get: $x - 2y + (x + 2y) = -2 + 10 \rightarrow 2x = 8 \rightarrow x = 4$. Now, substitute 4 for the x in the first equation: $4 - 2y = -2$. By solving this equation, $y = 3$
Example	What is the value of x and y in this system of equations? $\begin{cases} 3x - y = 7 \\ -x + 4y = 5 \end{cases}$ **Solution:** Solving System of Equations by Elimination: $\begin{array}{c} 3x - y = 7 \\ \hline -x + 4y = 5 \end{array}$ Multiply the second equation by 3, then add it to the first equation. $\begin{array}{c} 3x - y = 7 \\ 3(-x + 4y = 5) \end{array} \Rightarrow \begin{array}{c} 3x - y = 7 \\ -3x + 12y = 15) \end{array} \Rightarrow 11y = 22 \Rightarrow y = 2$. Now, substitute 2 for y in the first equation and solve for x. $3x - (2) = 7 \Rightarrow 3x = 9 \Rightarrow x = 3$
Your Turn!	1) $-4x + 4y = 8$ $\quad$ 2) $-5x + y = -3$ $ -4x + 2y = 6$ $\qquad\quad$ $3x - 8y = 24$ $\quad x = -1$ $\qquad\qquad\qquad$ $x = 0$ $\qquad\quad y = 1$ $\qquad\qquad\qquad\quad y = -3$ 3) $y = -2$ $\qquad\qquad$ 4) $y = -3x + 5$ $ 4x - 3y = 8$ $\qquad\quad$ $5x - 4y = -3$ $\quad x = \dfrac{1}{2}$ $\qquad\qquad\qquad$ $x = 1$ $\qquad\quad y = -2$ $\qquad\qquad\qquad y = 2$ 5) $20x - 18y = -26$ $\quad$ 6) $-9x - 12y = 15$ $ -10x + 6y = 22$ $\qquad\quad$ $2x - 6y = 14$ $\quad x = -4$ $\qquad\qquad\qquad$ $x = 1$ $\qquad\quad y = -3$ $\qquad\qquad\qquad y = -2$

Name:	Date: ....

Topic	**Graphing Single–Variable Inequalities**
Notes	✓ An inequality compares two expressions using an inequality sign. ✓ Inequality signs are: "less than" $<$, "greater than" $>$, "less than or equal to" $\leq$, and "greater than or equal to" $\geq$. ✓ To graph a single–variable inequality, find the value of the inequality on the number line. ✓ For less than ($<$) or greater than ($>$) draw open circle on the value of the variable. If there is an equal sign too, then use filled circle. ✓ Draw an arrow to the right for greater or to the left for less than.
Example	**Draw a graph for this inequality.** $x < 5$ **Solution:** Since, the variable is less than 5, then we need to find 5 in the number line and draw an open circle on it. Then, draw an arrow to the left.
Your Turn!	1) $x < 4$ 3) $x \geq -3$ 5) $x > -6$ 7) $-2 \leq x$ 	2) $x \geq -1$ 4) $x \leq 6$ 6) $2 > x$ 8) $x > 0$

Name:	Date: ....

Topic	Graphing Single–Variable Inequalities- Answers
Notes	✓ An inequality compares two expressions using an inequality sign. ✓ Inequality signs are: "less than" <, "greater than" >, "less than or equal to" ≤, and "greater than or equal to" ≥. ✓ To graph a single–variable inequality, find the value of the inequality on the number line. ✓ For less than (<) or greater than (>) draw open circle on the value of the variable. If there is an equal sign too, then use filled circle. ✓ Draw an arrow to the right for greater or to the left for less than.
Example	***Draw a graph for this inequality.*** $x < 5$ **Solution:** Since, the variable is less than 5, then we need to find 5 in the number line and draw an open circle on it. Then, draw an arrow to the left.
Your Turn!	1) $x < 4$ 2) $x \geq -1$ 3) $x \geq -3$ 4) $x \leq 6$ 5) $x > -6$ 6) $2 > x$ 7) $-2 \leq x$ 8) $x > 0$

Name:	Date: ....

Topic	One–Step Inequalities
Notes	✓ Inequality signs are: "less than" <, "greater than" >, "less than or equal to" ≤, and "greater than or equal to" ≥. ✓ You only need to perform one Math operation in order to solve the one-step inequalities. ✓ To solve one-step inequalities, find the inverse (opposite) operation is being performed. ✓ For dividing or multiplying both sides by negative numbers, flip the direction of the inequality sign.
Example	***Solve this inequality.*** $x + 12 < 60 \Rightarrow$ _____ Here, the operation is addition and its inverse operation is subtraction. To solve this inequality, subtract 12 from both sides of the ***inequality:*** $x + 12 - 12 < 60 - 12$ Then simplify: $x < 48$

Your Turn!	1) $4x < -8 \Rightarrow$ _____	2) $x + 6 > 28 \Rightarrow$ _____
	3) $-3x \geq 36 \Rightarrow$ _____	4) $x - 16 \leq 4 \Rightarrow$ _____
	5) $\frac{x}{2} \geq -9 \Rightarrow$ _____	6) $48 < 6x \Rightarrow$ _____
	7) $77 \leq 11x \Rightarrow$ _____	8) $\frac{x}{4} > 9 \Rightarrow$ _____

Name:	Date: ....

Topic	One–Step Inequalities - Answers	
Notes	✓ Inequality signs are: "less than" $<$, "greater than" $>$, "less than or equal to" $\leq$, and "greater than or equal to" $\geq$. ✓ You only need to perform one Math operation in order to solve the one-step inequalities. ✓ To solve one-step inequalities, find the inverse (opposite) operation is being performed. ✓ For dividing or multiplying both sides by negative numbers, flip the direction of the inequality sign.	
Example	**Solve this inequality.** $x + 12 < 60 \Rightarrow$ _____ Here, the operation is addition and its inverse operation is subtraction. To solve this inequality, subtract 12 from both sides of the **inequality:** $x + 12 - 12 < 60 - 12$ Then simplify: $x < 48$	
Your Turn!	1) $4x < -8 \Rightarrow x < -2$	2) $x + 6 > 28 \Rightarrow x > 22$
	3) $-3x \geq 36 \Rightarrow x \leq -12$	4) $x - 16 \leq 4 \Rightarrow x \leq 20$
	5) $\frac{x}{2} \geq -9 \Rightarrow x \geq -18$	6) $48 < 6x \Rightarrow 8 < x$
	7) $77 \leq 11x \Rightarrow 7 \leq x$	8) $\frac{x}{4} > 9 \Rightarrow x > 36$

Name:	Date: ....

Topic	**Multi –Step Inequalities**
Notes	✓ Isolate the variable. ✓ Simplify using the inverse of addition or subtraction. ✓ Simplify further by using the inverse of multiplication or division. ✓ For dividing or multiplying both sides by negative numbers, flip the direction of the inequality sign.
Example	***Solve this inequality.*** $3x + 12 \leq 21$ **Solution:** First subtract 12 from both sides: $3x + 12 - 12 \leq 21 - 12$ Then simplify: $3x + 12 - 12 \leq 21 - 12 \rightarrow 3x \leq 9$ Now divide both sides by 3: $\frac{3x}{3} \leq \frac{9}{3} \rightarrow x \leq 3$

Your Turn!	1) $5x + 6 < 36 \rightarrow$ _____	2) $2x - 8 \leq 6 \rightarrow$ _____
	3) $2x - 5 \leq 17 \rightarrow$ _____	4) $14 - 7x \geq -7 \rightarrow$ _____
	5) $18 - 6x \geq -6 \rightarrow$ _____	6) $2x - 18 \leq 16 \rightarrow$ _____
	7) $8 + 4x < 44 \rightarrow$ _____	8) $5 - 4x < 17 \rightarrow$ _____

Name:	Date: ....

Topic	**Multi –Step Inequalities - Answers**
Notes	✓ Isolate the variable. ✓ Simplify using the inverse of addition or subtraction. ✓ Simplify further by using the inverse of multiplication or division. ✓ For dividing or multiplying both sides by negative numbers, flip the direction of the inequality sign.
Example	***Solve this inequality.*** $3x + 12 \leq 21$ **Solution:** First subtract 12 from both sides: $3x + 12 - 12 \leq 21 - 12$ Then simplify: $3x + 12 - 12 \leq 21 - 12 \rightarrow 3x \leq 9$ Now divide both sides by 3: $\frac{3x}{3} \leq \frac{9}{3} \rightarrow x \leq 3$

Your Turn!	1) $5x + 6 < 36 \rightarrow x < 6$	2) $2x - 8 \leq 6 \rightarrow x \leq 7$
	3) $2x - 5 \leq 17 \rightarrow x \leq 11$	4) $14 - 7x \geq -7 \rightarrow x \leq 3$
	5) $18 - 6x \geq -6 \rightarrow x \leq 4$	6) $2x - 18 \leq 16 \rightarrow x \leq 17$
	7) $8 + 4x < 44 \rightarrow x < 9$	8) $5 - 4x < 17 \rightarrow x > -3$

Name:	Date: ....

Topic	**Finding Slope**
Notes	✓ The slope of a line represents the direction of a line on the coordinate plane. ✓ A line on coordinate plane can be drawn by connecting two points. ✓ To find the slope of a line, we need two points. ✓ The slope of a line with two points A (x_1, y_1) and B (x_2, y_2) can be found by using this formula: $\frac{y_2 - y_1}{x_2 - x_1} = \frac{rise}{run}$ ✓ The equation of a line is typically written as $y = mx + b$ where m is the slope and b is the y-intercept.
Examples	***Find the slope of the line through these two points:*** $(4, -12)$ *and* $(9, 8)$. **Solution:** Slope $= \frac{y_2 - y_1}{x_2 - x_1}$. Let (x_1, y_1) be $(4, -12)$ and (x_2, y_2) be $(9, 8)$. ***Then:*** slope $= \frac{y_2 - y_1}{x_2 - x_1} = \frac{8 - (-12)}{9 - 4} = \frac{8 + 12}{5} = \frac{20}{5} = 4$ ***Find the slope of the line with equation*** $y = 5x - 6$ **Solution:** when the equation of a line is written in the form of $y = mx + b$, the slope is m. In this line: $y = 5x - 6$, the slope is 5.
Your Turn!	1) $(2, 3), (4, 7)$ Slope = ____	2) $(-2, 2), (0, 4)$ Slope = ____
	3) $(4, -2), (2, 4)$ Slope = ____	4) $(-4, -1), (0, 7)$ Slope = ____
	5) $y = 3x + 18$ Slope = ____	6) $y = 12x - 3$ Slope = ____

Name:	Date: ....

Topic	**Finding Slope - Answers**
Notes	✓ The slope of a line represents the direction of a line on the coordinate plane. ✓ A line on coordinate plane can be drawn by connecting two points. ✓ To find the slope of a line, we need two points. ✓ The slope of a line with two points A (x_1, y_1) and B (x_2, y_2) can be found by using this formula: $\frac{y_2 - y_1}{x_2 - x_1} = \frac{rise}{run}$ ✓ The equation of a line is typically written as $y = mx + b$ where m is the slope and b is the y-intercept.
Examples	***Find the slope of the line through these two points:*** $(4, -12)$ *and* $(9, 8)$. **Solution:** Slope $= \frac{y_2 - y_1}{x_2 - x_1}$. Let (x_1, y_1) be $(4, -12)$ and (x_2, y_2) be $(9, 8)$. ***Then:*** slope $= \frac{y_2 - y_1}{x_2 - x_1} = \frac{8-(-1\ )}{9-4} = \frac{8+12}{5} = \frac{20}{5} = 4$ ***Find the slope of the line with equation*** $y = 5x - 6$ **Solution:** when the equation of a line is written in the form of $y = mx + b$, the slope is m. In this line: $y = 5x - 6$, the slope is 5.

Your Turn!	1) $(2,3), (4,7)$ Slope $= 2$	2) $(-2,2), (0,4)$ Slope $= 1$
	3) $(4,-2), (2,4)$ Slope $= -3$	4) $(-4,-1), (0,7)$ Slope $= 2$
	5) $y = 3x + 18$ Slope $= 3$	6) $y = 12x - 3$ Slope $= 12$

| Name: .... | Date: .... |

Topic	**Graphing Lines Using Slope–Intercept Form**
Notes	✓ Slope–intercept form of a line: given the slope m and the y–intercept (the intersection of the line and y-axis) b, then the equation of the line is: $$y = mx + b$$
Example	*Sketch the graph of* $y = -2\text{x} - 1$. **Solution:** To graph this line, we need to find two points. When x is zero the value of y is -1. And when y is zero the value of x is $-\frac{1}{2}$. $$x = 0 \rightarrow y = -2(0) - 1 = -1, y = 0 \rightarrow 0$$ $$= -2x - 1 \rightarrow x = -\frac{1}{2}$$ Now, we have two points: $(0, -1)$ and $(-\frac{1}{2}, 0)$. Find the points and graph the line. Remember that the slope of the line is $-\frac{1}{2}$.
Your Turn!	1) $y = -4x + 1$ 2) $y = -x - 5$

Name:	Date: ....

Topic	**Graphing Lines Using Slope–Intercept Form - Answers**
Notes	✓ Slope–intercept form of a line: given the slope **m** and the **y**–intercept (the intersection of the line and y-axis) **b**, then the equation of the line is: $$y = mx + b$$

Example	**Sketch the graph of** $y = -2x - 1$. **Solution:** To graph this line, we need to find two points. When x is zero the value of y is -1. And when y is zero the value of x is $-\frac{1}{2}$. $$x = 0 \rightarrow y = -2(0) - 1 = -1, y = 0 \rightarrow 0$$ $$= -2x - 1 \rightarrow x = -\frac{1}{2}$$ Now, we have two points: $(0, -1)$ and $(-\frac{1}{2}, 0)$. Find the points and graph the line. Remember that the slope of the line is $-\frac{1}{2}$.

Your Turn!	1) $y = -4x + 1$ 	2) $y = -x - 5$

Name:	Date: ....

Topic	Writing Linear Equations
Notes	✓ The equation of a line: $y = mx + b$ ✓ Identify the slope. ✓ Find the y–intercept. This can be done by substituting the slope and the coordinates of a point (x, y) on the line.
Example	**Write the equation of the line through $(3, 1)$ and $(-1, 5)$.** **Solution:** $Slop = \frac{y_2 - y_1}{x_2 - x_1} = \frac{5 - 1}{-1 - 3} = \frac{4}{-4} = -1 \rightarrow m = -1$ To find the value of b, you can use either points. The answer will be the same: $y = -x + b$ $(3, 1) \rightarrow 1 = -3 + b \rightarrow b = 4$ $(-1, 5) \rightarrow 5 = -(-1) + b \rightarrow b = 4$ The equation of the line is: $y = -x + 4$

Your Turn!	1) through: $(-2, 7), (1, 4)$ $y =$	2) through: $(6, 1), (5, 2)$ $y =$
	3) through: $(5, -1), (8, 2)$ $y =$	4) through: $(-2, 4), (4, -8)$ $y =$
	5) through: $(6, -5), (-5, 6)$ $y =$	6) through: $(4, -4), (-2, 8)$ $y =$
	7) through $(8, 8)$, Slope: 2 $y =$	8) through $(-7, 10)$, Slope: -2 $y =$

Name:	Date: ....

Topic	**Writing Linear Equations - Answers**	
Notes	✓ The equation of a line: $y = mx + b$ ✓ Identify the slope. ✓ Find the y–intercept. This can be done by substituting the slope and the coordinates of a point (x, y) on the line.	
Example	**Write the equation of the line through $(3, 1)$ and $(-1, 5)$.** **Solution:** $Slop = \frac{y_2 - y_1}{x_2 - x_1} = \frac{5 - 1}{-1 - 3} = \frac{4}{-4} = -1 \rightarrow m = -1$ To find the value of b, you can use either points. The answer will be the same: $y = -x + b$ $(3, 1) \rightarrow 1 = -3 + b \rightarrow b = 4$ $(-1, 5) \rightarrow 5 = -(-1) + b \rightarrow b = 4$ The equation of the line is: $y = -x + 4$	
Your Turn!	1) through: $(-2, 7), (1, 4)$ $y = -x + 5$	2) through: $(6, 1), (5, 2)$ $y = -x + 7$
	3) through: $(5, -1), (8, 2)$ $y = x - 6$	4) through: $(-2, 4), (4, -8)$ $y = -2x$
	5) through: $(6, -5), (-5, 6)$ $y = -x + 1$	6) through: $(4, -4), (-2, 8)$ $y = -2x + 4$
	7) through $(8, 8)$, Slope: 2 $y = 2x - 8$	8) through $(-7, 10)$, Slope: -2 $y = -2x - 4$

Name:	Date: ....

Topic	Finding Midpoint	
Notes	✓ The middle of a line segment is its midpoint. ✓ The Midpoint of two endpoints A (x_1, y_1) and B (x_2, y_2) can be found using this formula: $M(\frac{x_1+x_2}{2}, \frac{y_1+y_2}{2})$	
Example	Find the midpoint of the line segment with the given endpoints. $(1, -2), (3, 6)$ **Solution:** Midpoint $= (\frac{x_1+x_2}{2}, \frac{y_1+y_2}{2}) \rightarrow (x_1, y_1) = (1, -2)$ and $(x_2, y_2) = (3, 6)$ Midpoint $= (\frac{1+3}{2}, \frac{-2+6}{2}) \rightarrow (\frac{4}{2}, \frac{4}{2}) \rightarrow M(2, 2)$	
Your Turn!	1) $(6, 0), (-4, 2)$ *Midpoint* $= (\_\_, \_\_)$	2) $(4, -1), (2, 3)$ *Midpoint* $= (\_\_, \_\_)$
	3) $(-3, 4), (-5, 0)$ *Midpoint* $= (\_\_, \_\_)$	4) $(8, 1), (-4, 5)$ *Midpoint* $= (\_\_, \_\_)$
	5) $(6, 7), (-4, 5)$ *Midpoint* $= (\_\_, \_\_)$	6) $(2, -3), (2, 5)$ *Midpoint* $= (\_\_, \_\_)$
	7) $(7, 3), (-1, -7)$ *Midpoint* $= (\_\_, \_\_)$	8) $(3, 9), (-1, 5)$ *Midpoint* $= (\_\_, \_\_)$
	9) $(3, 4), (-7, -6)$ *Midpoint* $= (\_\_, \_\_)$	10) $(-5, 2), (11, -6)$ *Midpoint* $= (\_\_, \_\_)$

Name:	Date: ....

Topic	**Finding Midpoint - Answers**	
Notes	✓ The middle of a line segment is its midpoint. ✓ The Midpoint of two endpoints A (x_1, y_1) and B (x_2, y_2) can be found using this formula: $M(\frac{x_1+x_2}{2}, \frac{y_1+y_2}{2})$	
Example	Find the midpoint of the line segment with the given endpoints. $(\mathbf{1}, -\mathbf{2}), (\mathbf{3}, \mathbf{6})$ **Solution:** Midpoint $= (\frac{x_1+x_2}{2}, \frac{y_1+y_2}{2}) \rightarrow (x_1, y_1) = (1, -2)$ and $(x_2, y_2) = (3, 6)$ Midpoint $= (\frac{1+3}{2}, \frac{-2+6}{2}) \rightarrow (\frac{4}{2}, \frac{4}{2}) \rightarrow M(2, 2)$	
Your Turn!	1) $(6, 0), (-4, 2)$ ***Midpoint*** $= (1, 1)$	2) $(4, -1), (2, 3)$ ***Midpoint*** $= (3, 1)$
	3) $(-3, 4), (-5, 0)$ ***Midpoint*** $= (-4, 2)$	4) $(8, 1), (-4, 5)$ ***Midpoint*** $= (2, 3)$
	5) $(6, 7), (-4, 5)$ ***Midpoint*** $= (1, 6)$	6) $(2, -3), (2, 5)$ ***Midpoint*** $= (2, 1)$
	7) $(7, 3), (-1, -7)$ ***Midpoint*** $= (3, -2)$	8) $(3, 9), (-1, 5)$ ***Midpoint*** $= (1, 7)$
	9) $(3, 4), (-7, -6)$ ***Midpoint*** $= (-2, -1)$	10) $(-5, 2), (11, -6)$ ***Midpoint*** $= (3, -2)$

Name:	Date: ....

Topic	**Finding Distance of Two Points**
Notes	✓ Use this formula to find the distance of two points A (x_1, y_1) and B (x_2, y_2): $$d = \sqrt{(x_2 - x_1)^2 + (y_2 - y_1)^2}$$
Example	*Find the distance of two points* $(-1, 5)$ and $(4, -7)$. **Solution:** *Use distance of two points formula:* $d =$ $\sqrt{(x_2 - x_1)^2 + (y_2 - y_1)^2}$ $(x_1, y_1) = (-1, 5)$, and $(x_2, y_2) = (4, -7)$ Then: $d = \sqrt{(x_2 - x_1)^2 + (y_2 - y_1)^2} \rightarrow d =$ $\sqrt{(4 - (-1))^2 + (-7 - 5)^2} = \sqrt{(-5)^2 + (-12)^2} = \sqrt{25 + 144} =$ $\sqrt{169} = 13$

Your Turn!	1) $(6, 2), (-4, 2)$ **Distance** = ____	2) $(2, -3), (2, 5)$ **Distance** = ____
	3) $(-5, 10), (7, 1)$ **Distance** = ____	4) $(8, 1), (-4, 6)$ **Distance** = ____
	5) $(-3, 6), (-4, 5)$ **Distance** = ____	6) $(4, -1), (14, 23)$ **Distance** = ____
	7) $(-3, 4), (-5, 0)$ **Distance** = ____	8) $(3, 9), (-1, 5)$ **Distance** = ____

Name:	**Date:** ....

Topic	**Finding Distance of Two Points - Answers**
Notes	✓ Use this formula to find the distance of two points A (x_1, y_1) and B (x_2, y_2): $$d = \sqrt{(x_2 - x_1)^2 + (y_2 - y_1)^2}$$
Example	*Find the distance of two points* $(-1, 5)$ *and* $(4, -7)$. **Solution:** *Use distance of two points formula:* $d = \sqrt{(x_2 - x_1)^2 + (y_2 - y_1)^2}$ $(x_1, y_1) = (-1, 5)$, and $(x_2, y_2) = (4, -7)$ Then: $d = \sqrt{(x_2 - x_1)^2 + (y_2 - y_1)^2} \rightarrow d =$ $\sqrt{(4 - (-1))^2 + (-7 - 5)^2} = \sqrt{(-5)^2 + (-12)^2} = \sqrt{25 + 144} =$ $\sqrt{169} = 13$

Your Turn!	1) $(6, 2), (-4, 2)$ **Distance** $= 10$	2) $(2, -3), (2, 5)$ **Distance** $= 8$
	3) $(-5, 10), (7, 1)$ **Distance** $= 15$	4) $(8, 1), (-4, 6)$ **Distance** $= 13$
	5) $(-3, 6), (-4, 5)$ **Distance** $= \sqrt{2}$	6) $(4, -1), (14, 23)$ **Distance** $= 26$
	7) $(-3, 4), (-5, 0)$ **Distance** $= \sqrt{20} = 2\sqrt{5}$	8) $(3, 9), (-1, 5)$ **Distance** $= \sqrt{32} = 4\sqrt{2}$

| Name: .... | Date: .... |

Topic	**Multiplication Property of Exponents**
Notes	✓ Exponents are shorthand for repeated multiplication of the same number by itself. For example, instead of 2×2, we can write 2^2. For $3 \times 3 \times 3 \times 3$, we can write 3^4 ✓ In algebra, a variable is a letter used to stand for a number. The most common letters are: $x, y, z, a, b, c, m, and\ n$. ✓ Exponent's rules: $x^a \times x^b = x^{a+b}$, $\frac{x^a}{x^b} = x^{a-b}$ $\quad (x^a)^b = x^{a \times b} \qquad (xy)^a = x^a \times y^a \qquad (\frac{a}{b})^c = \frac{a^c}{b^c}$
Example	*Multiply.* $4x^3 \times 2x^2$ Use Exponent's rules: $x^a \times x^b = x^{a+b} \rightarrow x^3 \times x^2 = x^{3+2} = x^5$ Then: $4x^3 \times 2x^2 = 8x^5$
Your Turn!	1) $x^2 \times 3x =$ 2) $5x^4 \times x^2 =$ 3) $3x^2 \times 4x^5 =$ 4) $3x^2 \times 6xy =$ 5) $3x^5y \times 5x^2y^3 =$ 6) $3x^2y^2 \times 5x^2y^8 =$ 7) $5x^2y \times 5x^2y^7 =$ 8) $6x^6 \times 4x^9y^4 =$ 9) $8x^2y^5 \times 7x^5y^3 =$ 10) $12x^6x^2 \times 3xy^5 =$

| Name: .... | Date: .... |

Topic	**Multiplication Property of Exponents - Answers**
Notes	✓ Exponents are shorthand for repeated multiplication of the same number by itself. For example, instead of 2×2, we can write 2^2. For $3 \times 3 \times 3 \times 3$, we can write 3^4 ✓ In algebra, a variable is a letter used to stand for a number. The most common letters are: $x, y, z, a, b, c, m,$ and n. ✓ Exponent's rules: $x^a \times x^b = x^{a+b}$, $\frac{x^a}{x^b} = x^{a-b}$ $(x^a)^b = x^{a \times b}$ $\qquad (xy)^a = x^a \times y^a$ $\qquad (\frac{a}{b})^c = \frac{a^c}{b^c}$
Example	**Multiply.** $4x^3 \times 2x^2$ Use Exponent's rules: $x^a \times x^b = x^{a+b}$ → $x^3 \times x^2 = x^{3+2} = x^5$ Then: $4x^3 \times 2x^2 = 8x^5$
Your Turn!	1) $x^2 \times 3x = 3x^3$ 2) $5x^4 \times x^2 = 5x^6$ 3) $3x^2 \times 4x^5 = 12x^7$ 4) $3x^2 \times 6xy = 18x^3y$ 5) $3x^5y \times 5x^2y^3 = 15x^7y^4$ 6) $3x^2y^2 \times 5x^2y^8 = 15x^4y^{10}$ 7) $5x^2y \times 5x^2y^7 = 25x^4y^8$ 8) $6x^6 \times 4x^9y^4 = 24x^{15}y^4$ 9) $8x^2y^5 \times 7x^5y^3 = 56x^7y^8$ 10) $12x^6x^2 \times 3xy^5 = 36x^9y^5$

Name:	Date: ....

Topic	**Division Property of Exponents**
Notes	✓ For division of exponents use these formulas: $\frac{x^a}{x^b} = x^{a-b}$, $x \neq 0$ $\frac{x^a}{x^b} = \frac{1}{x^{b-a}}$, $x \neq 0$, $\frac{1}{x^b} = x^{-b}$
Example	**Simplify.** $\frac{6x^3y}{36x^2y^3}$ First cancel the common factor: $6 \rightarrow \frac{6x^3y}{36x^2y^3} = \frac{x^3y}{6x^2y^3}$ Use Exponent's rules: $\frac{x^a}{x^b} = x^{a-b} \rightarrow \frac{x^3}{x^2} = x^{3-2} = x^1 = x$ Then: $\frac{6x^3y}{36x^2y^3} = \frac{xy}{9y^3} \rightarrow$ now cancel the common factor: $y \rightarrow \frac{xy}{6y^3} = \frac{x}{6y^2}$
Your Turn!	1) $\frac{3^7}{3^2} =$ 2) $\frac{5x}{10x^3} =$ 3) $\frac{3x^3}{2x^5} =$ 4) $\frac{12x^3}{14x^6} =$ 5) $\frac{12x^3}{9y^8} =$ 6) $\frac{25xy^4}{5x^6y^2} =$ 7) $\frac{2x^4y^5}{7xy^2} =$ 8) $\frac{16x^2y^8}{4x^3} =$ 9) $\frac{12x^4}{15x^7y^9} =$ 10) $\frac{12yx^4}{10yx^8} =$

Name:	Date: ....

Topic	**Division Property of Exponents - Answers**	
Notes	✓ For division of exponents use following formulas: $\frac{x^a}{x^b} = x^{a-b}$, $x \neq 0$ $\frac{x^a}{x^b} = \frac{1}{x^{b-a}}$, $x \neq 0$, $\qquad \frac{1}{x^b} = x^{-b}$	
Example	*Simplify.* $\frac{6x^3y}{36x^2y^3}$ First cancel the common factor: $6 \rightarrow \frac{6x^3y}{36x^2y^3} = \frac{x^3y}{6x^2y^3}$ Use Exponent's rules: $\frac{x^a}{x^b} = x^{a-b} \rightarrow \frac{x^3}{x^2} = x^{3-2} = x^1 = x$ Then: $\frac{6x^3y}{36x^2y^3} = \frac{xy}{9y^3} \rightarrow$ now cancel the common factor: $y \rightarrow \frac{xy}{6y^3} = \frac{x}{6y^2}$	
Your Turn!	1) $\frac{3^7}{3^2} = 3^5$	2) $\frac{5x}{10x^3} = \frac{1}{2x^2}$
	3) $\frac{3x^3}{2x^5} = \frac{3}{2x^2}$	4) $\frac{12x^3}{14x^6} = \frac{6}{7x^3}$
	5) $\frac{12x^3}{9y^8} = \frac{4x^3}{3y^8}$	6) $\frac{25xy^4}{5x^6y^2} = \frac{5y^2}{x^5}$
	7) $\frac{2x^4y^5}{7xy^2} = \frac{2x^3y^3}{7}$	8) $\frac{16x^2y^8}{4x^3} = \frac{4y^8}{x}$
	9) $\frac{12x^4}{15x^7y^9} = \frac{4}{5x^3y^9}$	10) $\frac{12y^8x^4}{10y^2x^8} = \frac{6y^6}{5x^4}$

| Name: .... | Date: .... |

Topic	Powers of Products and Quotients	
Notes	✓ For any nonzero numbers a and b and any integer x, $$(ab)^x = a^x \times b^x, \quad \left(\frac{a}{b}\right)^c = \frac{a^c}{b^c}$$	
Example	**Simplify.** $\left(\frac{2x^3}{x}\right)^2$ First cancel the common factor: $x \rightarrow \left(\frac{2x^3}{x}\right)^2 = (2x^2)^2$ Use Exponent's rules: $(ab)^x = a^x \times b^x$ Then: $(2x^2)^2 = (2)^2(x^2)^2 = 4x^4$	
Your Turn!	1) $(4x^3x^3)^2 =$	2) $(3x^3 \times 5x)^2 =$
	3) $(10x^{11}y^3)^2 =$	4) $(9x^7y^5)^2 =$
	5) $(4x^4y^6)^3 =$	6) $(3x \times 4y^3)^2 =$
	7) $\left(\frac{5x}{x^2}\right)^2 =$	8) $\left(\frac{x^4y^4}{x^2y^2}\right)^3 =$
	9) $\left(\frac{25x}{5x^6}\right)^2 =$	10) $\left(\frac{x^8}{x^6y^2}\right)^2 =$

Name:	Date: ....

Topic	Powers of Products and Quotients - Answers	
Notes	✓ For any nonzero numbers a and b and any integer x, $$(ab)^x = a^x \times b^x, \left(\frac{a}{b}\right)^c = \frac{a^c}{b^c}$$	
Example	**Simplify.** $\left(\frac{2x^3}{x}\right)^2$ First cancel the common factor: $x \to \left(\frac{2x^3}{x}\right)^2 = \left(2x^2\right)^2$ Use Exponent's rules: $(ab)^x = a^x \times b^x$ Then: $\left(2x^2\right)^2 = (2)^2\left(x^2\right)^2 = 4x^4$	
Your Turn!	1) $(4x^3x^3)^2 = 16x^{12}$	2) $(3x^3 \times 5x)^2 = 225x^8$
	3) $(10x^{11}y^3)^2 = 100x^{22}y^6$	4) $(9x^7y^5)^2 = 81x^{14}y^{10}$
	5) $(4x^4y^6)^3 = 64\,x^{12}y^{18}$	6) $(3x \times 4y^3)^2 = 144x^2y^6$
	7) $\left(\frac{5x}{x^2}\right)^2 = \frac{25}{x^2}$	8) $\left(\frac{x^4y^4}{x^2y^2}\right)^3 = x^6y^6$
	9) $\left(\frac{25x}{5x^6}\right)^2 = \frac{25}{x^{10}}$	10) $\left(\frac{x^8}{x^6y^2}\right)^2 = \frac{x^4}{y^4}$

Name:	Date: ....

Topic	Zero and Negative Exponents
Notes	✓ A negative exponent is the reciprocal of that number with a positive exponent. $(3)^{-2} = \frac{1}{3^2}$ ✓ Zero-Exponent Rule: $a^0 = 1$, this means that anything raised to the zero power is 1. For example: $(28x^2 y)^0 = 1$
Example	*Evaluate.* $\left(\frac{1}{3}\right)^{-2} =$ Use negative exponent's rule: $\left(\frac{1}{x^a}\right)^{-2} = (x^a)^2 \rightarrow \left(\frac{1}{3}\right)^{-2} = (3)^2 =$ Then: $(3)^2 = 9$

Your Turn!	1) $2^{-3} =$	2) $3^{-3} =$
	3) $7^{-3} =$	4) $1^{-3} =$
	5) $8^{-3} =$	6) $4^{-4} =$
	7) $10^{-3} =$	8) $7^{-4} =$
	9) $\left(\frac{1}{8}\right)^{-1} =$	10) $\left(\frac{1}{5}\right)^{-2} =$

Name:	Date: ....

Topic	Zero and Negative Exponents - Answers	
Notes	✓ A negative exponent is the reciprocal of that number with a positive exponent. $(3)^{-2} = \frac{1}{3^2}$ ✓ Zero-Exponent Rule: $a^0 = 1$, this means that anything raised to the zero power is 1. For example: $(28x^2y)^0 = 1$	
Example	*Evaluate.* $\left(\frac{1}{3}\right)^{-2} =$ Use negative exponent's rule: $\left(\frac{1}{x^a}\right)^{-2} = (x^a)^2 \rightarrow \left(\frac{1}{3}\right)^{-2} = (3)^2 =$ Then: $(3)^2 = 9$	
Your Turn!	1) $2^{-3} = \frac{1}{8}$	2) $3^{-3} = \frac{1}{27}$
	3) $7^{-3} = \frac{1}{343}$	4) $1^{-3} = 1$
	5) $8^{-3} = \frac{1}{512}$	6) $4^{-4} = \frac{1}{256}$
	7) $10^{-3} = \frac{1}{1,000}$	8) $7^{-4} = \frac{1}{2,401}$
	9) $\left(\frac{1}{8}\right)^{-1} = 8$	10) $\left(\frac{1}{5}\right)^{-2} = 25$

Name:	Date: ....

Topic	**Negative Exponents and Negative Bases**	
Notes	✓ Make the power positive. A negative exponent is the reciprocal of that number with a positive exponent. ✓ The parenthesis is important! 5^{-2} is not the same as $(-5)^{-2}$ $$(-5)^{-2} = -\frac{1}{5^2} \text{ and } (-5)^{-2} = +\frac{1}{5^2}$$	
Example	***Simplify.*** $\left(-\frac{3x}{4yz}\right)^{-2} =$ Use negative exponent's rule: $\left(\frac{x^a}{x^b}\right)^{-2} = \left(\frac{x^b}{x^a}\right)^2 \rightarrow \left(-\frac{3x}{4yz}\right)^{-3} = \left(-\frac{4yz}{3x}\right)^3$ Now use exponent's rule: $\left(\frac{a}{b}\right)^c = \frac{a^c}{b^c} \rightarrow \left(-\frac{4yz}{3x}\right)^3 = \frac{4^3 y^3 z^3}{3^3 x^3} = \frac{64 y^3 z^3}{27 x^3}$	
Your Turn!	1) $-5x^{-2}y^{-3} =$	2) $20x^{-4}y^{-1} =$
	3) $14a^{-6}b^{-7} =$	4) $-12x^2 y^{-3} =$
	5) $-\dfrac{25}{x^{-6}} =$	6) $\dfrac{7b}{-9c^{-4}} =$
	7) $\dfrac{7ab}{a^{-3}b^{-1}} =$	8) $-\dfrac{5n^{-2}}{10p^{-3}} = -$
	9) $\dfrac{4ab^{-2}}{-3c^{-2}} =$	10) $\left(\dfrac{3a}{2c}\right)^{-2} =$

Name:	Date: ....

Topic	**Negative Exponents and Negative Bases - Answers**
Notes	✓ Make the power positive. A negative exponent is the reciprocal of that number with a positive exponent. ✓ The parenthesis is important! ✓ 5^{-2} is not the same as $(-5)^{-2}$ $\quad (-5)^{-2} = -\frac{1}{5^2}$ and $(-5)^{-2} = +\frac{1}{5^2}$
Example	*Simplify.* $\left(-\frac{3x}{4yz}\right)^{-2} =$ Use negative exponent's rule: $\left(\frac{x^a}{x^b}\right)^{-2} = \left(\frac{x^b}{x^a}\right)^2 \rightarrow \left(-\frac{3x}{4yz}\right)^{-3} = \left(-\frac{4yz}{3x}\right)^3$ Now use exponent's rule: $\left(\frac{a}{b}\right)^c = \frac{a^c}{b^c} \rightarrow \left(-\frac{4yz}{3x}\right)^3 = \frac{4^3 y^3 z^3}{3^3 x^3} = \frac{64y^3 z^3}{27x^3}$

Your Turn!	$1) -5x^{-2}y^{-3} = -\frac{5}{x^2\,y^3}$	$2)\ 20x^{-4}y^{-1} = \frac{20}{x^4 y}$
	$3)\ 14a^{-6}b^{-7} = \frac{14}{a^6 b^7}$	$4)\ -12x^2 y^{-3} = -\frac{12x^2}{y^3}$
	$5)\ -\frac{25}{x^{-6}} = -25x^6$	$6)\ \frac{7b}{-9c^{-4}} = -\frac{7bc^4}{9}$
	$7)\ \frac{7ab}{a^{-3}b^{-1}} = 7a^4 b^2$	$8)\ -\frac{5n^{-2}}{10p^{-3}} = -\frac{p^3}{2n^2}$
	$9)\ \frac{4ab^{-2}}{-3c^{-2}} = -\frac{4ac^2}{3b^2}$	$10)\ \left(\frac{3a}{2c}\right)^{-2} = \frac{4c^2}{9a^2}$

Name:	Date: ....

Topic	**Scientific Notation**
Notes	✓ It is used to write very big or very small numbers in decimal form. ✓ In scientific notation all numbers are written in the form of: $m \times 10^n$ **Decimal notation** — **Scientific notation** 3 — 3×10^0 $-45{,}000$ — -4.5×10^4 0.3 — 3×10^{-1} $2{,}122.456$ — 2.122456×10^3
Example	***Write 0.00054 in scientific notation.*** First, move the decimal point to the right so that you have a number that is between 1 and 10. Then: $m = 5.4$ Now, determine how many places the decimal moved in step 1 by the power of 10. Then: 10^{-4} → When the decimal moved to the right, the exponent is negative. Then: $0.00054 = 5.4 \times 10^{-4}$

Your Turn!

1) $0.000325 =$	2) $0.000023 =$
3) $52{,}000{,}000 =$	4) $21{,}000 =$
5) $3 \times 10^{-1} =$	6) $5 \times 10^{-2} =$
7) $1.2 \times 10^3 =$	8) $2 \times 10^{-4} =$

Name:	Date: ....

Topic	**Scientific Notation - Answers**	
Notes	✓ It is used to write very big or very small numbers in decimal form. ✓ In scientific notation all numbers are written in the form of: $$m \times 10^n$$ <table><tr><td>**Decimal notation**</td><td>**Scientific notation**</td></tr><tr><td>3</td><td>3×10^0</td></tr><tr><td>$-45,000$</td><td>-4.5×10^4</td></tr><tr><td>0.3</td><td>3×10^{-1}</td></tr><tr><td>2,122.456</td><td>2.122456×10^3</td></tr></table>	
Example	**Write 0.00054 in scientific notation.** First, move the decimal point to the right so that you have a number that is between 1 and 10. Then: $m = 5.4$ Now, determine how many places the decimal moved in step 1 by the power of 10. Then: 10^{-4} → When the decimal moved to the right, the exponent is negative. Then: $0.00054 = 5.4 \times 10^{-4}$	
Your Turn!	1) $0.000325 = 3.25 \times 10^{-4}$	2) $0.00023 = 2.3 \times 10^{-5}$
	3) $52,000,000 = 5.2 \times 10^7$	4) $21,000 = 2.1 \times 10^4$
	5) $3 \times 10^{-1} = 0.3$	6) $5 \times 10^{-2} = 0.05$
	7) $1.2 \times 10^3 = 1,200$	8) $2 \times 10^{-4} = 0.0002$

Name:	Date: ....

Topic	Radicals

Notes	✓ If n is a positive integer and x is a real number, then: $\sqrt[n]{x} = x^{\frac{1}{n}}$, $\sqrt[n]{xy} = x^{\frac{1}{n}} \times y^{\frac{1}{n}}$, $\sqrt[n]{\frac{x}{y}} = \frac{x^{\frac{1}{n}}}{y^{\frac{1}{n}}}$, and $\sqrt[n]{x} \times \sqrt[n]{y} = \sqrt[n]{xy}$ ✓ A square root of x is a number r whose square is: $r^2 = x$ (r is a square root of x. ✓ To add and subtract radicals, we need to have the same values under the radical. For example: $\sqrt{3} + \sqrt{3} = 2\sqrt{3}$, $3\sqrt{5} - \sqrt{5} = 2\sqrt{5}$
Example	*Evaluate.* $\sqrt{32} + \sqrt{8} =$ **Solution:** Since we do not have the same values under the radical, we cannot add these two radicals. But we can simplify each radical. $\sqrt{32} = \sqrt{16} \times \sqrt{2} = 4\sqrt{2}$ and $\sqrt{8} = \sqrt{4} \times \sqrt{2} = 2\sqrt{2}$ Now, we have the same values under the radical. Then: $$\sqrt{32} + \sqrt{8} = 4\sqrt{2} + 2\sqrt{2} = 6\sqrt{2}$$
Your Turn!	1) $\sqrt{9} \times \sqrt{9} =$ 2) $\sqrt{8} \times \sqrt{2} =$ 3) $\sqrt{3} \times \sqrt{27} =$ 4) $\sqrt{32} \div \sqrt{2} =$ 5) $\sqrt{2} + \sqrt{8} =$ 6) $\sqrt{27} - \sqrt{3} =$ 7) $4\sqrt{5} - 2\sqrt{5} =$ 8) $3\sqrt{3} \times 2\sqrt{3} =$

| Name: .... | Date: .... |

Topic	**Radicals - Answers**
Notes	✓ If n is a positive integer and x is a real number, then: $\sqrt[n]{x} = x^{\frac{1}{n}}$, $\sqrt[n]{xy} = x^{\frac{1}{n}} \times y^{\frac{1}{n}}$, $\sqrt[n]{\frac{x}{y}} = \frac{x^{\frac{1}{n}}}{y^{\frac{1}{n}}}$, and $\sqrt[n]{x} \times \sqrt[n]{y} = \sqrt[n]{xy}$ ✓ A square root of x is a number r whose square is: $\boldsymbol{r^2 = x}$ ($\boldsymbol{r}$ is a square root of $\boldsymbol{x}$. ✓ To add and subtract radicals, we need to have the same values under the radical. For example: $\sqrt{3} + \sqrt{3} = 2\sqrt{3}$, $3\sqrt{5} - \sqrt{5} = 2\sqrt{5}$
Example	***Evaluate.*** $\sqrt{32} + \sqrt{8} =$ **Solution:** Since we do not have the same values under the radical, we cannot add these two radicals. But we can simplify each radical. $\sqrt{32} = \sqrt{16} \times \sqrt{2} = 4\sqrt{2}$ and $\sqrt{8} = \sqrt{4} \times \sqrt{2} = 2\sqrt{2}$ Now, we have the same values under the radical. Then: $$\sqrt{32} + \sqrt{8} = 4\sqrt{2} + 2\sqrt{2} = 6\sqrt{2}$$

Your Turn!	1) $\sqrt{9} \times \sqrt{9} = 9$	2) $\sqrt{8} \times \sqrt{2} = 4$
	3) $\sqrt{3} \times \sqrt{27} = 9$	4) $\sqrt{32} \div \sqrt{2} = 4$
	5) $\sqrt{2} + \sqrt{8} = 3\sqrt{2}$	6) $\sqrt{27} - \sqrt{3} = 2\sqrt{3}$
	7) $4\sqrt{5} - 2\sqrt{5} = 2\sqrt{5}$	8) $3\sqrt{3} \times 2\sqrt{3} = 18$

Name:	Date: ....

Topic	**Simplifying Polynomials**	
Notes	✓ Find "like" terms. (they have same variables with same power). ✓ Use "FOIL". (First–Out–In–Last) for binomials: $$(x + a)(x + b) = x^2 + (b + a)x + ab$$ ✓ Add or Subtract "like" terms using order of operation.	
Example	**Simplify this expression.** $(x + 3)(x - 8) =$ **Solution:** First apply FOIL method: $(a + b)(c + d) = ac + ad + bc + bd$ $(x + 3)(x - 8) = x^2 - 8x + 3x - 24$ Now combine like terms: $x^2 - 8x + 3x - 24 = x^2 - 5x - 24$	
Your Turn!	1) $-(2x - 4) =$ _____	2) $2(2x + 6) =$ _____
	3) $3x(3x - 4) =$ _____	4) $5x(2x + 8) =$ _____
	5) $-2x(5x + 6) + 5x =$ _____	6) $-4x(8x - 3) - x^2 =$ _____
	7) $(x + 4)(x + 5) =$ _____	8) $(x + 2)(x + 8) =$ _____
	9) $-4x^2 + 10x^3 + 5x^2 =$ _____	10) $-3x^5 + 10x^4 + 5x^5 =$ _____

Name:	Date: ....

Topic	**Simplifying Polynomials - Answers**	
Notes	✓ Find "like" terms. (they have same variables with same power). ✓ Use "FOIL". (First–Out–In–Last) for binomials: $$(x + a)(x + b) = x^2 + (b + a)x + ab$$ ✓ Add or Subtract "like" terms using order of operation.	
Example	*Simplify this expression*. $(x + 3)(x - 8) =$ **Solution:** First apply FOIL method: $(a + b)(c + d) = ac + ad + bc + bd$ $(x + 3)(x - 8) = x^2 - 8x + 3x - 24$ Now combine like terms: $x^2 - 8x + 3x - 24 = x^2 - 5x - 24$	
Your Turn!	1) $-(2x - 4) =$ $-2x + 4$	2) $2(2x + 6) =$ $4x + 12$
	3) $3x(3x - 4) =$ $9x^2 - 12x$	4) $5x(2x + 8) =$ $10x^2 + 40x$
	5) $-2x(5x + 6) + 5x =$ $-10x^2 - 7x$	6) $-4x(8x - 3) - x^2 =$ $-33x^2 + 12x$
	7) $(x + 4)(x + 5) =$ $x^2 + 9x + 20$	8) $(x + 2)(x + 8) =$ $x^2 + 10x + 16$
	9) $-4x^2 + 10x^3 + 5x^2 =$ $10x^3 + x^2$	10) $-3x^5 + 10x^4 + 5x^5 =$ $2x^5 + 10x^4$

Name: ………………………………….	Date: …………………………………

Topic	**Adding and Subtracting Polynomials**
Notes	✓ Adding polynomials is just a matter of combining like terms, with some order of operations considerations thrown in. ✓ Be careful with the minus signs, and don't confuse addition and multiplication!
Example	***Simplify the expressions.*** $(3x^2 - 4x^3) - (5x^3 - 8x^2) =$ **Solution:** First use Distributive Property: $-(5x^3 - 8x^2) = -5x^3 + 8x^2$ $\rightarrow (3x^2 - 4x^3) - (5x^3 - 8x^2) = 3x^2 - 4x^3 - 5x^3 + 8x^2$ Now combine like terms: $3x^2 - 4x^3 - 5x^3 + 8x^2 = -9x^3 + 11x^2$

Your Turn!	1) $(x^2 - x) + (4x^2 - 5) =$ _____	2) $(2x^3 + x) - (x^3 + 2) =$ _____
	3) $(x^2 - 5x) + (6x^2 - 5) =$ _____	4) $(8x^2 - 2) - (3x^2 + 7) =$ _____
	5) $(3x^2 + 2) - (2 - 4x^2) =$ _____	6) $(x^3 + x^2) - (x^3 - 10) =$ _____
	7) $(3x^3 - 2x) - (x - x^3) =$ _____	8) $(x - 5x^4) - (2x^4 + 3x) =$ _____
	9) $(6x^3 + 5) - (4 - 5x^3) =$ _____	10) $(2x^2 + 5x^3) - (6x^3 + 7) =$ _____

Name:	Date: ....

Topic	**Adding and Subtracting Polynomials - Answers**
Notes	✓ Adding polynomials is just a matter of combining like terms, with some order of operations considerations thrown in. ✓ Be careful with the minus signs, and don't confuse addition and multiplication!
Example	*Simplify the expressions.* $(3x^2 - 4x^3) - (5x^3 - 8x^2) =$ **Solution:** First use Distributive Property: $-(5x^3 - 8x^2) = -5x^3 + 8x^2$ $\rightarrow (3x^2 - 4x^3) - (5x^3 - 8x^2) = 3x^2 - 4x^3 - 5x^3 + 8x^2$ Now combine like terms: $3x^2 - 4x^3 - 5x^3 + 8x^2 = -9x^3 + 11x^2$

Your Turn!	1) $(x^2 - x) + (4x^2 - 5) =$ $5x^2 - x - 5$	2) $(2x^3 + x) - (x^3 + 2) =$ $x^3 + x - 2$
	3) $(x^2 - 5x) + (6x^2 - 5) =$ $7x^2 - 5x - 5$	4) $(8x^2 - 2) - (3x^2 + 7) =$ $5x^2 - 9$
	5) $(3x^2 + 2) - (2 - 4x^2) =$ $7x^2$	6) $(x^3 + x^2) - (x^3 - 10) =$ $x^2 + 10$
	7) $(3x^3 - 2x) - (x - x^3) =$ $4x^3 - 3x$	8) $(x - 5x^4) - (2x^4 + 3x) =$ $7x^4 - 2x$
	9) $(6x^3 + 5) - (4 - 5x^3) =$ $11x^3 + 1$	10) $(2x^2 + 5x^3) - (6x^3 + 7) =$ $-x^3 + 2x^2 - 7$

Name: ....   **Date:** ....

Topic	Multiplying Binomials
Notes	✓ A binomial is a polynomial that is the sum or the difference of two terms, each of which is a monomial. ✓ To multiply two binomials, use "FOIL" method. (First–Out–In–Last) $(x + a)(x + b) = x \times x + x \times b + a \times x + a \times b = x^2 + bx + ax + ab$
Example	*Multiply.* $(x - 4)(x + 9) =$ **Solution:** Use "FOIL". (First–Out–In–Last): $(x - 4)(x + 9) = x^2 + 9x - 4x - 36$ Then simplify: $x^2 + 9x - 4x - 36 = x^2 + 5x - 36$

Your Turn!	1) $(x + 2)(x + 2) =$ _____	2) $(x + 3)(x + 2) =$ _____
	3) $(x - 3)(x + 4) =$ _____	4) $(x - 2)(x - 4) =$ _____
	5) $(x + 3)(x + 4) =$ _____	6) $(x + 5)(x + 4) =$ _____
	7) $(x - 6)(x - 5) =$ _____	8) $(x - 5)(x - 5) =$ _____
	9) $(x + 6)(x - 8) =$ _____	10) $(x - 9)(x + 7) =$ _____

Name: ………………………………..	Date: ……………………………………

Topic	**Multiplying Binomials - Answers**
Notes	✓ A binomial is a polynomial that is the sum or the difference of two terms, each of which is a monomial. ✓ To multiply two binomials, use "FOIL" method. (First–Out–In–Last) $(x + a)(x + b) = x \times x + x \times b + a \times x + a \times b = x^2 + bx + ax + ab$
Example	**Multiply.** $(x - 4)(x + 9) =$ **Solution:** Use "FOIL". (First–Out–In–Last): $(x - 4)(x + 9) = x^2 + 9x - 4x - 36$ Then simplify: $x^2 + 9x - 4x - 36 = x^2 + 5x - 36$

Your Turn!	1) $(x + 2)(x + 2) =$ $x^2 + 4x + 4$	2) $(x + 3)(x + 2) =$ $x^2 + 5x + 6$
	3) $(x - 3)(x + 4) =$ $x^2 + x - 12$	4) $(x - 2)(x - 4) =$ $x^2 - 6x + 8$
	5) $(x + 3)(x + 4) =$ $x^2 + 7x + 12$	6) $(x + 5)(x + 4) =$ $x^2 + 9x + 20$
	7) $(x - 6)(x - 5) =$ $x^2 - 11x + 30$	8) $(x - 5)(x - 5) =$ $x^2 - 10x + 25$
	9) $(x + 6)(x - 8) =$ $x^2 - 2x - 48$	10) $(x - 9)(x + 7) =$ $x^2 - 2x - 63$

Name:	Date: ....

Topic	**Multiplying and Dividing Monomials**	
Notes	✓ When you divide or multiply two monomials you need to divide or multiply their coefficients and then divide or multiply their variables. ✓ In case of exponents with the same base, you need to subtract their powers. ✓ Exponent's rules: $$x^a \times x^b = x^{a+b}, \qquad \frac{x^a}{x^b} = x^{a-b}$$ $$\frac{1}{x^b} = x^{-b}, \quad (x^a)^b = x^{a \times b}$$ $$(xy)^a = x^a \times y^a$$	
Example	***Divide expressions.*** $\frac{-18x^5 y^6}{2xy^2} =$ **Solution:** Use exponents' division rule: $\frac{x^a}{x^b} = x^{a-b}, \frac{x^5}{x} = x^{5-1} = x^4$ and $\frac{y^6}{y^2} = y^4$ Then: $\frac{-18x^5 y^6}{2xy^2} = -9x^4 y^4$	
Your Turn!	1) $(x^8 y)(xy^2) =$ _____	2) $(x^4 y^3)(x^2 y^3) =$ _____
	3) $(x^7 y^4)(2x^5 y^2) =$ _____	4) $(3x^5 y^4)(4x^6 y^3) =$ _____
	5) $(-6x^8 y^7)(4x^6 y^9) =$ _____	6) $(-2x^9 y^3)(9x^7 y^8) =$ _____
	7) $\frac{30x^8 y^9}{6x^5 y^4} =$ _____	8) $\frac{-42x^{12} y^{16}}{7x^8 y^9} =$ _____

Name:	Date: ....

Topic	**Multiplying and Dividing Monomials - Answers**	
Notes	✓ When you divide or multiply two monomials you need to divide or multiply their coefficients and then divide or multiply their variables. ✓ In case of exponents with the same base, you need to subtract their powers. ✓ Exponent's rules: $$x^a \times x^b = x^{a+b}, \qquad \frac{x^a}{x^b} = x^{a-b}$$ $$\frac{1}{x^b} = x^{-b}, \quad (x^a)^b = x^{a \times b}$$ $$(xy)^a = x^a \times y^a$$	
Example	**Divide expressions.** $\frac{-18x^5y^6}{2xy^2} =$ **Solution:** Use exponents' division rule: $\frac{x^a}{x^b} = x^{a-b}, \frac{x^5}{x} = x^{5-1} = x^4$ and $\frac{y^6}{y^2} = y^4$ Then: $\frac{-18x^5y^6}{2xy^2} = -9x^4y^4$	
Your Turn!	1) $(x^8y)(xy^2) =$ x^9y^3	2) $(x^4y^3)(x^2y^3) =$ x^6y^6
	3) $(x^7y^4)(2x^5y^2) =$ $2x^{12}y^6$	4) $(3x^5y^4)(4x^6y^3) =$ $12x^{11}y^7$
	5) $(-6x^8y^7)(4x^6y^9) =$ $-24x^{14}y^{16}$	6) $(-2x^9y^3)(9x^7y^8) =$ $-18x^{16}y^{11}$
	7) $\frac{30x^8y^9}{6x^5y^4} =$ $5x^3y^5$	8) $\frac{-42x^{12}y^{16}}{7x^8y^9} =$ $-6x^4y^7$

Name:	Date: ....

Topic	Multiplying a Polynomial and a Monomial
Notes	✓ When multiplying monomials, use the product rule for exponents. $x^a \times x^b = x^{a+b}$ ✓ When multiplying a monomial by a polynomial, use the distributive property. $$a \times (b + c) = a \times b + a \times c = ab + ac$$ $$a \times (b - c) = a \times b - a \times c = ab - ac$$
Example	*Multiply expressions.* $4x(5x - 8) =$ **Solution:** Use Distributive Property: $4x(5x - 8) = 4x \times 5x - 4x \times (8) =$ Now, simplify: $4x \times 5x - 4x \times (8) = 20x^2 - 32x$

Your Turn!	1) $3x(2x + y) =$ _____	2) $x(x - 3y) =$ _____
	3) $-x(5x - 3y) =$ _____	4) $4x(x + 5y) =$ _____
	5) $-x(5x + 8y) =$ _____	6) $2x(6x - 7y) =$ _____
	7) $-3x(x^3 + 4y^2 - 6x) =$ _____	8) $7x(x^2 - 5y^2 + 4) =$ _____

Name:	Date: ....

Topic	**Multiplying a Polynomial and a Monomial - Answers**	
Notes	✓ When multiplying monomials, use the product rule for exponents. $x^a \times x^b = x^{a+b}$ ✓ When multiplying a monomial by a polynomial, use the distributive property. $$a \times (b + c) = a \times b + a \times c = ab + ac$$ $$a \times (b - c) = a \times b - a \times c = ab - ac$$	
Example	**Multiply expressions.** $4x(5x - 8) =$ **Solution:** Use Distributive Property: $4x(5x - 8) = 4x \times 5x - 4x \times (8) =$ Now, simplify: $4x \times 5x - 4x \times (8) = 20x^2 - 32x$	
Your Turn!	1) $3x(2x + y) =$ $6x^2 + 3xy$	2) $x(x - 3y) =$ $x^2 - 3xy$
	3) $-x(5x - 3y) =$ $-5x^2 + 3xy$	4) $4x(x + 5y) =$ $4x^2 + 20xy$
	5) $-x(5x + 8y) =$ $-5x^2 - 8xy$	6) $2x(6x - 7y) =$ $12x^2 - 14xy$
	7) $-3x(x^3 + 4y^2 - 6x) =$ $-3x^4 - 12xy^2 + 18x^2$	8) $7x(x^2 - 5y^2 + 4) =$ $7x^3 - 35xy^2 + 28x$

Name:	Date: ....

Topic	**Multiplying Monomials**
Notes	✓ A monomial is a polynomial with just one term: Examples: $\boldsymbol{5x}$ or $\boldsymbol{7x^2yz^8}$. ✓ When you multiply monomials, first multiply the coefficients (a number placed before and multiplying the variable) and then multiply the variables using multiplication property of exponents. $x^a \times x^b = x^{a+b}$
Example	*Multiply.* $(-3xy^4z^5) \times (2x^2y^5z^3) =$ **Solution:** Multiply coefficients and find same variables and use multiplication property of exponents: $x^a \times x^b = x^{a+b}$ $-3 \times 2 = -6$, $x \times x^2 = x^{1+2} = x^3$, $y^4 \times y^5 = y^{4+5} = y^9$, and $z^2 \times z^5 = z^{2+5} = z^7$ Then: $(-3xy^4z^5) \times (2x^2y^5z^3) = -6x^3y^9z^7$
Your Turn!	1) $2x^2 \times 4x^6 =$ _____ 2) $5x^7 \times 6x^4 =$ _____ 3) $-2x^2y^4 \times 6x^3y^2 =$ _____ 4) $-5x^5y \times 3x^3y^4 =$ _____ 5) $8x^7y^5 \times 5x^6y^3 =$ _____ 6) $-6x^7y^5 \times (-3x^9y^8) =$ _____ 7) $12x^8y^8z^4 \times 3x^4y^3z =$ _____ 8) $-8x^9y^7z^{11} \times 7x^6y^7z^5 =$ _____

Name:	Date: ....

Topic	**Multiplying Monomials**
Notes	✓ A monomial is a polynomial with just one term: Examples: $5x$ or $7x^2yz^8$. ✓ When you multiply monomials, first multiply the coefficients (a number placed before and multiplying the variable) and then multiply the variables using multiplication property of exponents. $x^a \times x^b = x^{a+b}$
Example	**Multiply.** $(-3xy^4z^5) \times (2x^2y^5z^3) =$ **Solution:** Multiply coefficients and find same variables and use multiplication property of exponents: $x^a \times x^b = x^{a+b}$ $-3 \times 2 = -6$, $x \times x^2 = x^{1+2} = x^3$, $y^4 \times y^5 = y^{4+5} = y^9$, and $z^2 \times z^5 = z^{2+5} = z^7$ Then: $(-3xy^4z^5) \times (2x^2y^5z^3) = -6x^3y^9z^7$

Your Turn!	1) $2x^2 \times 4x^6 =$ $\quad 8x^8$	2) $5x^7 \times 6x^4 =$ $\quad 30x^{11}$
	3) $-2x^2y^4 \times 6x^3y^2 =$ $\quad -12x^5y^6$	4) $-5x^5y \times 3x^3y^4 =$ $\quad -15x^8y^5$
	5) $8x^7y^5 \times 5x^6y^3 =$ $\quad 40x^{13}y^8$	6) $-6x^7y^5 \times (-3x^9y^8) =$ $\quad 18x^{16}y^{13}$
	7) $12x^8y^8z^4 \times 3x^4y^3z =$ $36x^{12}y^{11}z^5$	8) $-8x^9y^7z^{11} \times 7x^6y^7z^5 =$ $-56x^{15}y^{14}z^{16}$

Name:	Date: ....

Topic	Factoring Trinomials
Notes	To factor trinomial, use of the following methods: ✓ "FOIL": $(x + a)(x + b) = x^2 + (b + a)x + ab$ ✓ "Difference of Squares": $$a^2 - b^2 = (a + b)(a - b)$$ $$a^2 + 2ab + b^2 = (a + b)(a + b)$$ $$a^2 - 2ab + b^2 = (a - b)(a - b)$$ ✓ "Reverse FOIL": $x^2 + (b + a)x + ab = (x + a)(x + b)$
Example	**Factor this trinomial.** $x^2 + 12x + 32 =$ **Solution:** Break the expression into groups: $(x^2 + 4x) + (8x + 32)$ Now factor out x from $x^2 + 4x$: $x(x + 4)$, and factor out 8 from $8x + 32$: $8(x + 4)$ Then: $(x^2 + 4x) + (8x + 32) = x(x + 4) + 8(x + 4)$ Now factor out like term: $(x + 4) \rightarrow (x + 4)(x + 8)$

	1) $x^2 + 6x + 9 =$ _____	2) $x^2 + 5x + 6 =$ _____
	3) $x^2 + x + 12 =$ _____	4) $x^2 - 6x + 8 =$ _____
Your Turn!	5) $x^2 + 7x + 12 =$ _____	6) $x^2 + 12x + 32 =$ _____
	7) $x^2 - 11x + 30 =$ _____	8) $x^2 - 14x + 45 =$ _____

Name:	Date: ....

Topic	**Factoring Trinomials - Answers**
Notes	To factor trinomial, use of the following methods: ✓ "FOIL": $(x + a)(x + b) = x^2 + (b + a)x + ab$ ✓ "Difference of Squares": $$a^2 - b^2 = (a + b)(a - b)$$ $$a^2 + 2ab + b^2 = (a + b)(a + b)$$ $$a^2 - 2ab + b^2 = (a - b)(a - b)$$ ✓ "Reverse FOIL": $x^2 + (b + a)x + ab = (x + a)(x + b)$
Example	**Factor this trinomial**. $x^2 + 12x + 32 =$ **Solution:** Break the expression into groups: $(x^2 + 4x) + (8x + 32)$ Now factor out x from $x^2 + 4x : x(x + 4)$, and factor out 8 from $8x + 32$: $8(x + 4)$ Then: $(x^2 + 4x) + (8x + 32) = x(x + 4) + 8(x + 4)$ Now factor out like term: $(x + 4) \rightarrow (x + 4)(x + 8)$

Your Turn!	1) $x^2 + 6x + 9 =$ $(x + 3)(x + 3)$	2) $x^2 + 5x + 6 =$ $(x + 3)(x + 2)$
	3) $x^2 + x + 12 =$ $(x - 3)(x + 4)$	4) $x^2 - 6x + 8 =$ $(x - 2)(x - 4)$
	5) $x^2 + 7x + 12 =$ $(x + 3)(x + 4)$	6) $x^2 + 12x + 32 =$ $(x + 8)(x + 4)$
	7) $x^2 - 11x + 30 =$ $(x - 6)(x - 5)$	8) $x^2 - 14x + 45 =$ $(x - 9)(x - 5)$

| Name: .... | Date: .... |

Topic	**The Pythagorean Theorem**
Notes	✓ In any right triangle: $a^2 + b^2 = c^2$
Example	Right triangle ABC (not shown) has two legs of lengths 18 cm (AB) and 24 cm (AC). What is the length of the third side (BC)? **Solution:** Use Pythagorean Theorem: $a^2 + b^2 = c^2$ Then: $a^2 + b^2 = c^2 \rightarrow 18^2 + 24^2 = c^2 \rightarrow 324 + 576 = c^2$ $c^2 = 900 \rightarrow c = \sqrt{900} = 30\ cm$
Your Turn!	1) _____ 15, ?, 8 2) _____ 34, 16, ? 3) _____ 13, 5, ? 4) _____ 15, ?, 12

Name:	Date: ....

Topic	**The Pythagorean Theorem - Answers**	
Notes	✓ In any right triangle: $a^2 + b^2 = c^2$	
Example	Right triangle ABC (not shown) has two legs of lengths 18 cm (AB) and 24 cm (AC). What is the length of the third side (BC)? **Solution:** Use Pythagorean Theorem: $a^2 + b^2 = c^2$ Then: $a^2 + b^2 = c^2 \rightarrow 18^2 + 24^2 = c^2 \rightarrow 324 + 576 = c^2$ $c^2 = 900 \rightarrow c = \sqrt{900} = 30\ cm$	
Your Turn!	1) 17	2) 30
	3) 12	4) 9

Name:	Date: ....

Topic	**Triangles**
Notes	✓ In any triangle the sum of all angles is 180 degrees. ✓ Area of a triangle = $\frac{1}{2}$ ($base \times height$)
Example	**What is the area of the following triangle?** **Solution:** Use the area formula: Area = $\frac{1}{2}$ ($base \times height$) $base = 16$ and $height = 6$ Area = $\frac{1}{2}(16 \times 6) = \frac{96}{2} = 48$
Your Turn!	5) _____ 6) _____ 7) _____ 8) _____

Name:	Date: ....

Topic	**Triangles - Answers**
Notes	✓ In any triangle the sum of all angles is 180 degrees. ✓ Area of a triangle = $\frac{1}{2}$ $(base \times height)$
Example	**What is the area of the following triangle?** **Solution:** Use the area formula: Area = $\frac{1}{2}$ $(base \times height)$ $base = 16$ and $height = 6$ Area = $\frac{1}{2}(16 \times 6) = \frac{96}{2} = 48$
Your Turn!	5) 120 6) 252 7) 300 8) 736

Name:	Date: ....

Topic	**Polygons**
Notes	Perimeter of a square $= 4 \times side = 4s$ Perimeter of a rectangle $= 2(width + length)$ Perimeter of trapezoid $= a + b + c + d$ Perimeter of a regular hexagon $= 6a$ Perimeter of a parallelogram $= 2(l + w)$
Example	**Find the perimeter of following regular hexagon.** **Solution:** Since the hexagon is regular, all sides are equal. Then: Perimeter of Hexagon $= 6 \times (one\ side)$ Perimeter of Hexagon $= 6 \times (one\ side) = 6 \times 9 = 54\ m$

Your Turn!

9) *(rectangle)* _____

9 *in*

15 *in*

10) _____

8 m

10 m   10 m

14 m

11)   *(regular hexagon)* 5 m _____

12)   *(parallelogram)*_____

10 *in*

16 *in*

Name:	Date: ....

Topic	**Polygons - Answers**
Notes	Perimeter of a square $= 4 \times side = 4s$ Perimeter of a rectangle $= 2(width + length)$ Perimeter of trapezoid $= a + b + c + d$ Perimeter of a regular hexagon $= 6a$ Perimeter of a parallelogram $= 2(l + w)$

Example	**Find the perimeter of following regular hexagon.** **Solution:** Since the hexagon is regular, all sides are equal. Then: Perimeter of Hexagon $= 6 \times (one\ side)$ Perimeter of Hexagon $= 6 \times (one\ side) = 6 \times 9 = 54\ m$

Your Turn!	9) *(rectangle)* 48 *in* 9 *in* 15 *in*	10) 42 *m* 8 m 10 *m* 10 *m* 14 *m*
	11) *(regular hexagon)* 30 *m* 5 *m*	12) *(parallelogram)* 52 *in* 10 *in* 16 *in*

Name: ....   **Date:** ....

Topic	Circles
Notes	✓ In a circle, variable r is usually used for the radius and d for diameter and π is about 3.14. ✓ *Area of a circle* $= \pi r^2$ ✓ *Circumference of a circle* $= 2\pi r$
Example	**Find the area of the circle.** **Solution:** Use area formula: *Area* $= \pi r^2$ $r = 2\ in \rightarrow Area = \pi(2)^2 = 4\pi,\ \pi = 3.14$ **Then:** *Area* $= 4 \times 3.14 = 12.56\ in^2$
Your Turn!	**Find the area of each circle.** ($\pi = 3.14$) 1) _____ 2) _____ **Find the Circumference of each circle.** ($\pi = 3.14$) 3) _____ 4) _____

| Name: .... | Date: .... |

Topic	**Circles - Answers**
Notes	✓ In a circle, variable r is usually used for the radius and d for diameter and π is about 3.14. ✓ *Area of a circle* $= \pi r^2$ ✓ *Circumference of a circle* $= 2\pi r$ r
Example	**Find the area of the circle.** Solution: Use area formula: $Area = \pi r^2$ $r = 2\ in \rightarrow Area = \pi(2)^2 = 4\pi, \pi = 3.14$ **Then:** $Area = 4 \times 3.14 = 12.56\ in^2$ $2\ in$
Your Turn!	**Find the area of each circle.** $(\pi = 3.14)$ 1) $113.04\ cm^2$ $\qquad$ 2) $314\ in^2$ $6\ cm$ $\qquad$ $10\ in$ **Find the Circumference of each circle.** $(\pi = 3.14)$ 3) $50.24\ cm$ $\qquad$ 4) $37.68\ m$ $8\ cm$ $\qquad$ $6\ m$

Name:	Date: ....

Topic	Cubes
Notes	✓ A cube is a three-dimensional solid object bounded by six square sides. ✓ Volume is the measure of the amount of space inside of a solid figure, like a cube, ball, cylinder or pyramid. ✓ Volume of a cube $= (one\ side)^3$ ✓ surface area of cube $= 6 \times (one\ side)^2$
Example	***Find the volume and surface area of the following cube.*** 15 cm **Solution:** Use volume formula: $volume = (one\ side)^3$ Then: $volume = (one\ side)^3 = (15)^3 = 3,375\ cm^3$ Use surface area formula: $surface\ area\ of\ cube: 6(one\ side)^2 = 6(15)^2 = 6(225) = 1,350\ cm^2$
Your Turn!	***Find the volume of each cube.*** 1) _____ 11 in 2) _____ 13 ft 3) _____ 14 cm 4) _____ 30 m

Name:	Date: ....

Topic	**Cubes - Answers**
Notes	✓ A cube is a three-dimensional solid object bounded by six square sides. ✓ Volume is the measure of the amount of space inside of a solid figure, like a cube, ball, cylinder or pyramid. ✓ Volume of a cube $= (one\ side)^3$ ✓ surface area of cube $= 6 \times (one\ side)^2$
Example	***Find the volume and surface area of the following cube.*** $15\ cm$ **Solution:** Use volume formula: $volume = (one\ side)^3$ Then: $volume = (one\ side)^3 = (15)^3 = 3,375\ cm^3$ Use surface area formula: $surface\ area\ of\ cube: 6(one\ side)^2 = 6(15)^2 = 6(225) = 1,350\ cm^2$
Your Turn!	***Find the volume of each cube.*** 1) $1,331\ in^3$ $11\ in$ 2) $2,197\ ft^3$ $13\ ft$ 3) $2,744\ cm^3$ $14\ cm$ 4) $27,000\ m^3$ $30\ m$

Name: ....   **Date:** ....

Topic	Trapezoids
Notes	✓ A quadrilateral with at least one pair of parallel sides is a trapezoid. ✓ Area of a trapezoid $= \frac{1}{2}h(b_1 + b_2)$

Example

Calculate the area of the trapezoid.

   Solution:

Use area formula: $A = \frac{1}{2}h(b_1 + b_2)$

$b_1 = 8\ cm$, $b_2 = 12\ cm$ and $h = 14\ cm$

Then: $A = \frac{1}{2}(14)(12 + 8) = 7(20) = 140\ cm^2$

Your Turn!

1) _____

5 cm
4 cm
9 cm

2) _____

8 m
10 m
12 m

3) _____

7 ft
6 ft
15 ft

4) _____

10 cm
8 cm
14 cm

Name:	Date: ....

Topic	**Trapezoids - Answers**
Notes	✓ A quadrilateral with at least one pair of parallel sides is a trapezoid. ✓ Area of a trapezoid $= \frac{1}{2}h(b_1 + b_2)$

Example	**Calculate the area of the trapezoid.**
	  Solution:
	  Use area formula: $A = \frac{1}{2}h(b_1 + b_2)$
	  $b_1 = 8\ cm$, $b_2 = 12\ cm$ and $h = 14\ cm$
	  Then: $A = \frac{1}{2}(14)(12 + 8) = 7(20) = 140\ cm^2$

Your Turn!

1) $28\ cm^2$

2) $100\ m^2$

3) $66\ ft^2$

4) $96\ cm^2$

Name:	Date: ....

Topic	**Rectangular Prisms**	
Notes	✓ A solid 3-dimensional object which has six rectangular faces. ✓ Volume of a Rectangular prism $= \boldsymbol{Length \times Width \times Height}$ $Volume = l \times w \times h$ $Surface\ area = 2(wh + lw + lh)$	

Example

Find the volume and surface area of rectangular prism.
Solution:
Use volume formula: $Volume = l \times w \times h$

Then: $Volume = 4 \times 2 \times 6 = 48\ m^3$

Use surface area formula: $Surface\ area = 2(wh + lw + lh)$

Then: $Surface\ area = 2\big((2 \times 6) + (4 \times 2) + (4 \times 6)\big)$

$= 2(12 + 8 + 24) = 2(44) = 88\ m^2$

(4 m, 6 m, 2 m)

Your Turn!

Find the surface area of each Rectangular Prism.

1) _____
6 ft, 10 ft, 4 ft

2) _____
8 cm, 16 cm, 6 cm

3) _____
12 m, 18 m, 10 m

4) _____
20 in, 15 in, 12 in

Name:	Date: ....

Topic	**Rectangular Prisms - Answers**
Notes	✓ A solid 3-dimensional object which has six rectangular faces. ✓ Volume of a Rectangular prism = **Length × Width × Height** $Volume = l \times w \times h$ $Surface\ area = 2(wh + lw + lh)$
Example	***Find the volume and surface area of rectangular prism.*** **Solution:** Use volume formula: $Volume = l \times w \times h$ Then: $Volume = 4 \times 2 \times 6 = 48\ m^3$ Use surface area formula: $Surface\ area = 2(wh + lw + lh)$ Then: $Surface\ area = 2\big((2 \times 6) + (4 \times 2) + (4 \times 6)\big)$ $= 2(12 + 8 + 24) = 2(44) = 88\ m^2$
Your Turn!	**Find the surface area of each Rectangular Prism.** 1) $248\ ft^2$ 6 ft, 10 ft, 4 ft 2) $544\ cm^2$ 8 cm, 16 cm, 6 cm 3) $1,032\ m^2$ 12 m, 18 m, 10 m 4) $1,440\ in^2$ 20 in, 15 in, 12 in

Name:	Date: ....

Topic	**Cylinder**
Notes	✓ A cylinder is a solid geometric figure with straight parallel sides and a circular or oval cross section. ✓ *Volume of Cylinder Formula* $= \pi(radius)^2 \times height$ $\pi = 3.14$ ✓ *Surface area of a cylinder* $= 2\pi r^2 + 2\pi rh$ height radius
Example	**Find the volume and Surface area of the follow Cylinder.** **Solution:** Use volume formula: $Volume = \pi(radius)^2 \times height$ Then: $Volume = \pi(3)^2 \times 12 = 9\pi \times 12 = 108\pi$ $\pi = 3.14$ **then:** $Volume = 108\pi = 339.12 \ cm^3$ Use surface area formula: $Surface \ area = 2\pi r^2 + 2\pi rh$ **Then:** $2\pi(3)^2 + 2\pi(3)(12) = 2\pi(9) + 2\pi(36) = 18\pi + 72\pi = 90\pi$ $\pi = 3.14$ **Then:** $Surface \ area = 90 \times 3.14 = 282.6 \ cm^2$ 12 cm 3 cm
Your Turn!	**Find the volume of each Cylinder.** ($\pi = 3.14$) 1) _____ 2) _____ 10 in 2 in 14 m 5 m **Find the Surface area of each Cylinder.** ($\pi = 3.14$) 3) _____ 4) _____ 15 ft 9 ft 20 cm 12 cm

Name:	Date: ....

Topic	Cylinder - Answers
Notes	✓ A cylinder is a solid geometric figure with straight parallel sides and a circular or oval cross section. ✓ *Volume of Cylinder Formula* $= \pi(radius)^2 \times height$ $\pi = 3.14$ ✓ *Surface area of a cylinder* $= 2\pi r^2 + 2\pi rh$ *height* *radius*
Example	**Find the volume and Surface area of the follow Cylinder.** **Solution:** Use volume formula: $Volume = \pi(radius)^2 \times height$ Then: $Volume = \pi(3)^2 \times 12 = 9\pi \times 12 = 108\pi$ $\pi = 3.14$ **then:** $Volume = 108\pi = 339.12\ cm^3$ Use surface area formula: $Surface\ area = 2\pi r^2 + 2\pi rh$ **Then:** $2\pi(3)^2 + 2\pi(3)(12) = 2\pi(9) + 2\pi(36) = 18\pi + 72\pi = 90\pi$ $\pi = 3.14$ **Then:** $Surface\ area = 90 \times 3.14 = 282.6\ cm^2$ *12 cm* *3 cm*
Your Turn!	**Find the volume of each Cylinder.** ($\pi = 3.14$) 1) $125.6\ in^3$ 2) $1,099\ m^3$ *10 in* *2 in* *14 m* *5 m* **Find the Surface area of each Cylinder.** ($\pi = 3.14$) 3) $1,356.48\ ft^2$ 4) $2,411.52\ cm^2$ *15 ft* *9 ft* *20 cm* *12 cm*

Name:	Date: ....

Topic	**Mean, Median, Mode, and Range of the Given Data**
Notes	✓ Mean: $\dfrac{sum\ of\ the\ data}{total\ number\ of\ data\ entires}$ ✓ Mode: value in the list that appears most often. ✓ Median: is the middle number of a group of numbers that have been arranged in order by size. ✓ Range: the difference of largest value and smallest value in the list.
Example	***Find the mode and median of these numbers?*** $16, 10, 6, 3, 1, 16, 2, 4$ **Solution:** Mode: value in the list that appears most often. Number 16 is the value in the list that appears most often (there are two number 16). To find median, write the numbers in order: $1, 2, 3, 4, 6, 10, 16, 16$ Number 4 and 6 are in the middle. Find their average: $\dfrac{4+6}{2} = \dfrac{10}{2} = 5$ The median is 5.
Your Turn!	1) $3, 2, 4, 8, 3, 10$ Mode: _____ Range: _____ Mean: _____ Median: _____ 2) $6, 3, 2, 9, 5, 7, 2, 14$ Mode: _____ Range: _____ Mean: _____ Median: _____ 3) $5, 4, 3, 2, 9, 5, 6, 8, 12$ Mode: _____ Range: _____ Mean: _____ Median: _____ 4) $12, 6, 8, 6, 9, 6, 4, 13$ Mode: _____ Range: _____ Mean: _____ Median: _____

Name:	Date: ....

Topic	**Mean, Median, Mode, and Range of the Given Data - Answers**
Notes	✓ Mean: $\dfrac{sum\ of\ the\ data}{total\ number\ of\ data\ entires}$ ✓ Mode: value in the list that appears most often. ✓ Median: is the middle number of a group of numbers that have been arranged in order by size. ✓ Range: the difference of largest value and smallest value in the list.
Example	***Find the mode and median of these numbers?*** $16, 10, 6, 3, 1, 16, 2, 4$ **Solution:** Mode: value in the list that appears most often. Number 16 is the value in the list that appears most often (there are two number 16). To find median, write the numbers in order: $1, 2, 3, 4, 6, 10, 16, 16$ Number 4 and 6 are in the middle. Find their average: $\dfrac{4+6}{2} = \dfrac{10}{2} = 5$ The median is 5.

Your Turn!	1) $3, 2, 4, 8, 3, 10$ Mode: 3 Range: 8 Mean: 5 Median: 3.5	2) $6, 3, 2, 9, 5, 7, 2, 14$ Mode: 2 Range: 12 Mean: 6 Median: 5.5
	3) $5, 4, 3, 2, 9, 5, 6, 8, 12$ Mode: 5 Range: 10 Mean: 6 Median: 5	4) $12, 6, 8, 6, 9, 6, 4, 13$ Mode: 6 Range: 9 Mean: 8 Median: 7

Name:	Date: ....

Topic	**Probability Problems**
Notes	✓ Probability is the likelihood of something happening in the future. It is expressed as a number between zero (can never happen) to 1 (will always happen). ✓ Probability can be expressed as a fraction, a decimal, or a percent. ✓ Probability formula: $Probability = \frac{number\ of\ desired\ outcomes}{number\ of\ total\ outcomes}$
Example	***If there are 3 green balls, 4 red balls, and 10 blue balls in a basket, what is the probability that Jason will pick out a red ball from the basket?*** **Solution:** There are 4 red ball and 17 are total number of balls. Therefore, probability that Jason will pick out a red ball from the basket is 4 out of 17 or $\frac{4}{3+4+10} = \frac{4}{17}$
Your Turn!	1) A number is chosen at random from 1 to 20. Find the probability of selecting a prime number. (A prime number is a whole number that is only divisible by itself and 1) _____ 2) There are only red and blue cards in a box. The probability of choosing a red card in the box at random is one third. If there are 24 blue cards, how many cards are in the box? _____ 3) A die is rolled, what is the probability that an even number is obtained? _____

Name: .... | Date: ....

Topic	**Probability Problems - Answers**
Notes	✓ Probability is the likelihood of something happening in the future. It is expressed as a number between zero (can never happen) to 1 (will always happen). ✓ Probability can be expressed as a fraction, a decimal, or a percent. ✓ Probability formula: $Probability = \dfrac{number\ of\ desired\ outcomes}{number\ of\ total\ outcomes}$
Example	*If there are 3 green balls, 4 red balls, and 10 blue balls in a basket, what is the probability that Jason will pick out a red ball from the basket?* **Solution:** There are 4 red ball and 17 are total number of balls. Therefore, probability that Jason will pick out a red ball from the basket is 4 out of 17 or $\dfrac{4}{3+4+10} = \dfrac{4}{17}$
Your Turn!	1) A number is chosen at random from 1 to 20. Find the probability of selecting a prime number. (A prime number is a whole number that is only divisible by itself and 1) $\dfrac{8}{20} = \dfrac{2}{5}$ *(There are 8 prime numbers from 1 to 20: 2, 3, 5, 7, 11, 13, 17, 19)*
	2) There are only red and blue cards in a box. The probability of choosing a red card in the box at random is one third. If there are 24 blue cards, how many cards are in the box? 36
	3) A die is rolled, what is the probability that an even number is obtained? $\dfrac{1}{2}$

| Name: .... | Date: .... |

Topic	Pie Graph
Notes	✓ A Pie Chart is a circle chart divided into sectors, each sector represents the relative size of each value.

| **Example** | A library has 460 books that include Mathematics, Physics, Chemistry, English and History. Use following graph to answer the question.

What is the number of Physics books?
Solution: Number of total books = 460
Percent of Physics books = 25% = 0.25
Then, umber of Physics books:
$$0.25 \times 460 = 115$$ |

Your Turn!	The circle graph below shows all Mr. Smith's expenses for last month. Mr. Smith spent $440 for clothes last month. Mr. Smith's last month expenses
	1) How much did Mr. Smith spend for his Books last month? _____ 2) How much did Mr. Smith spend for Bills last month? _____ 3) How much did Mr. Smith spend for his foods last month? _____

Name:	Date: ....

Topic	**Pie Graph**	
Notes	✓ A Pie Chart is a circle chart divided into sectors, each sector represents the relative size of each value.	
Example	A library has 460 books that include Mathematics, Physics, Chemistry, English and History. Use following graph to answer the question. **What is the number of Physics books?** **Solution:** Number of total books = 460 Percent of Physics books = 25% = 0.25 Then, umber of Physics books: $$0.25 \times 460 = 115$$	History 10% English 15% Mathematics 30% Chemistry 20% Physics 25%
Your Turn!	The circle graph below shows all Mr. Smith's expenses for last month. Mr. Smith spent $440 for clothes last month. Foods 25% Bills 18% Others 23% Clothes 20% Books 14% Mr. Smith's last month expenses	
	1) How much did Mr. Smith spend for his Books last month? $308 2) How much did Mr. Smith spend for Bills last month? $396 3) How much did Mr. Smith spend for his foods last month? $550	

| Name: .... | Date: .... |

Topic	**Permutations and Combinations**
Notes	✓ Permutations: The number of ways to choose a sample of k elements from a set of n distinct objects where order does matter, and replacements are not allowed. For a permutation problem, use this formula: $$_nP_k = \frac{n!}{(n-k)!}$$ ✓ Combination: The number of ways to choose a sample of r elements from a set of n distinct objects where order does not matter, and replacements are not allowed. For a combination problem, use this formula: $$_nC_r = \frac{n!}{r!\,(n-r)!}$$ ✓ Factorials are products, indicated by an exclamation mark. For example, 4! Equals: $4 \times 3 \times 2 \times 1$. Remember that 0! is defined to be equal to 1.
Example	***How many ways can we pick a team of 4 people from a group of 8?*** **Solution:** Since the order doesn't matter, we need to use combination formula where n is 8 and r is 4. Then: $\frac{n!}{r!\,(n-r)!} = \frac{8!}{4!\,(8-4)!} = \frac{8!}{4!\,(4)!} = \frac{8\times7\times6\times5\times4!}{4!\,(4)!} = \frac{8\times7\times6\times5}{4\times3\times2\times1} = \frac{1,680}{24} = 70$
Your Turn!	1) In how many ways can 8 athletes be arranged in a straight line? _____
	2) How many ways can we award a first and second place prize among eight contestants? _____
	3) In how many ways can we choose 3 players from a team of 9 players? _____

Name:	Date: ....

Topic	**Permutations and Combinations - Answers**
Notes	✓ Permutations: The number of ways to choose a sample of k elements from a set of n distinct objects where order does matter, and replacements are not allowed. For a permutation problem, use this formula: $$_nP_k = \frac{n!}{(n-k)!}$$ ✓ Combination: The number of ways to choose a sample of r elements from a set of n distinct objects where order does not matter, and replacements are not allowed. For a combination problem, use this formula: $$_nC_r = \frac{n!}{r!\,(n-r)!}$$ ✓ Factorials are products, indicated by an exclamation mark. For example, 4! Equals: $4 \times 3 \times 2 \times 1$. Remember that 0! is defined to be equal to 1.
Example	***How many ways can we pick a team of 4 people from a group of 8?*** **Solution:** Since the order doesn't matter, we need to use combination formula where n is 8 and r is 4. Then: $\frac{n!}{r!\,(n-r)!} = \frac{8!}{4!\,(8-4)!} = \frac{8!}{4!\,(4)!} = \frac{8 \times 7 \times 6 \times 5 \times 4!}{4!\,(4)!} = \frac{8 \times 7 \times 6 \times 5}{4 \times 3 \times 2 \times 1} = \frac{1,680}{24} = 70$
Your Turn!	1) In how many ways can 8 athletes be arranged in a straight line? 40,320
	2) How many ways can we award a first and second place prize among eight contestants? 56
	3) In how many ways can we choose 3 players from a team of 9 players? 84

www.EffortlessMath.com

... So Much More Online!

✓ FREE Math lessons

✓ More Math learning books!

✓ Mathematics Worksheets

✓ Online Math Tutors

Need a PDF version of this book?

Visit www.EffortlessMath.com

Receive the PDF version of this book or get another FREE book!

Thank you for using our Book!

Do you LOVE this book?

Then, you can get the PDF version of this book or another book absolutely FREE!

Please email us at:

info@EffortlessMath.com

for details.

Made in United States
North Haven, CT
27 May 2022

19599254R00078